I0474126

The *Failure* of
Acquisition
Based Economics?

and *Desperate* Need for
Distribution
Based Economics

By:
LENARD LATIMER, JR.

Copyright © 2010 Lenard Latimer, Jr.
All rights reserved.

ISBN: 1470022028
ISBN 13: 9781470022020

Library of Congress Control Number: 2012910832
CreateSpace, North Charleston, SC

DEDICATION

This book is dedicated to my family and the children of the world. It is my attempt to relieve them of the tremendous debt, visionless governments, and polluted environment that we leave them. It is an apology for the crippled world we have left them. It is a blueprint to end government manipulations, relieve and stabilize our global economy. This book seeks to remove physical currency from our lives, businesses, and politics. It is also written to seek their forgiveness for squandering natural resources and ruining their lives by infecting them with our time tested hatreds and prejudices! With this book, and the help of God, I hope that a better world will be our lasting legacy to them.

CONTENTS

It is eloquently stated by *Ambrose*, the magnificent fourth-century bishop of Milan, who thundered:

"Think you, that you commit no injustice by keeping to yourself alone what would be the means of life to many. It is the bread of the hungry you cling to; it is the clothing of the naked you lock up; the money you bury is the redemption of the poor."

"A man's mind, stretched by new ideas, can never go back to its original dimensions."

Oliver W. Holmes

As we manipulate ourselves toward global economic collapse, and stand at the precipice of global, economically driven, political revolutions, we must take this moment in history to save ourselves from ourselves; by building an economic system to replace the one we now use which was derived from happenstance and the business and political manipulations of men! A working economy must benefit everyone and be free of the influences of politics, corporate power, race, gender, or religion! It must be stronger than the people that desire to wield our economies awesome power.

-Author-

As Countries of the World Are Going Door To Door
With Their Hands Out… Real Change

Can Only Come Through
Economic Evolution!

In an era of great scientific discovery, man-made medical miracles, crushing global hunger, growing global poverty, curable pain, and exploding global crime; isn't it time to replace our over manipulated, archaic, and dying economic system with something new and all encompassing? The economic paradigm put forth in this book will satisfy all sides of the political economic debate! It will end taxes and provide a global safety net for 7.5 billion people. It will allow for social upkeep and the expansion of our infrastructure without the use of a single tax dollar!

Chapter 1

LET'S START THE CONVERSATION

Our nation is ready to move forward and there is a desperate need for us to start the conversation! Americans are taking to the streets protesting everything from economic unfairness to social morals. Our economy is connected to every protest, movement, and cause that we have. The stalemates in our local, state, and federal governments, caused by fundamental differences, have driven some elected officials to obstruct the very governments they swore to serve. Some want to dismantle the social progress made over the last sixty years so we can turn more millionaires into billionaires.. Every election is an opportunity for us to move the country forward or back. It is an opportunity to define America as progressive and problem solving, or defeatist. This election we need to give our government a mandate to move America forward!

In our quest to achieve a stable society we must first complete a doctorate course I like to call Living 101. It is not taught in any college classroom and can only be achieved when we create a natural living environment for the entire human race! This book is about us creating a natural environment like those of other creatures in nature. An harmonious environment where each member has the potential to fulfill their productive potential, personal aspirations, and American dreams. We need a social economic environment that is designed for all mankind to participate in it and depend upon it.

<u>*SOCIALISM*</u>! There I said it. In this book you will find capitalistic ideals as well as ideals that are socialist because they both exist in every society. Our capitalistic ideals concern our personal drive, ambition, competitiveness, values, and the measurements of our individual productivity. Our socialist ideals concern things that apply to our society as a whole. To provide for our governments, public education systems, public transportation, energy, infrastructure expansion, and repair are some of our socialist

1

goals. Most of you have never talked about economic evolution either; but you will read about it here. Many of you who scream socialism, do so without even knowing what socialism is! You say socialism as if it were a dirty word. For those not sure about the meaning of the world socialism, it is defined as: 1. **a political system of communal ownership, a political theory or system in which the means of production and distribution are controlled by the people and operated according to equity and fairness rather than market principles.** Anybody see anything wrong with that! Socialism puts people first!

2. **movement based on socialism typically advocating an end to private property and to the exploitation of workers.** *An end to private property?* Really? I have never seen an armored car following a hearse! The end of private property ends at the grave. The illusion of "ownership" and "private property" will be discussed throughout this book. It is this illusion that keeps us trapped in a failed acquisition based economic system. We are producers and users of what we produce. Because ours is a system of acquisition we fool ourselves into thinking that we own the things we purchase to use.

3. **stage between capitalism and communism in Marxist theory, the stage after the proletarian revolution when a society is changing from capitalism to communism, marked by pay distributed according to work done rather than need.**

This last one, I believe, is a totally self serving statement intended to paint socialism as a pathway to communism, as marijuana has been painted as a pathway to hard drugs. The part about pay being distributed according to work done rather than need; is essentially calling for a fair economic system. As for socialism all of our systems are social because we are beings living in a **SOCIETY**... "social iety"! That being said, this book is intended to start a discussion about building a permanent social economic system designed to encompass the economic lives of every person in an ever growing global population.

Mankind is now standing on the precipice of another failing acquisition based economic system. Throughout history acquisition based economic systems have ended with social upheaval. All revolutions have ever accomplished was to replace one aristocracy with another. As long as the wealthy are content to watch the suffering of millions of people while they hoard wealth they will never spend, we will never be successful as civilization builders. When are we going to stop playing numbers games and create a permanent economy that allows everyone to participate in it; from the cradle to the grave?

We are mortal beings! Ownership, political power, and astronomical bank accounts, are just illusions we use to make us feel that we are in control of our lives. For many, who achieve financial success, they feel obligated to pursue political power to justify their greatness, rather than seeking to serve a calling to help humanity. These politicians are not easy to see, for most of us, and even harder to weed out! None of the politicians we send to Washington leave with less money than they had when they got there. With the exception of the Egyptian politicians, who really tried to take it with them, we will, eventually, leave this life with only the clothes on our backs.

There is a single protagonist in this tale of humanities struggle for economic permanence. Our greatest enemy is the physical currency we love to fold and put in our pocket. The folding money that some of us worship, is the bane, (or Bain in some cases) of our economic existence. We are facing a *global* economic crisis and anyone who thinks that we are not economically linked to every country in the world, in this floundering economy, is a fool. There is no turning back the clock to an earlier economic paradigm, as many would have us believe. We cannot protect ourselves from the economic collapses of other nations by retreating behind our shores. What worked for a hundred million Americans will not work for three hundred million Americans tied to seven billion people around the globe. People are looking to America for leadership and direction; after all, it was our leadership and direction that got the world to this point. What worked for a global population of four billion people after WWII with the Marshal Plan, will not work for seven and a half billion people. From here we must _all_ move forward or face economic extinction together. Don't think that Americas' sophistication and civility will spare us from the social uprisings and government upheavals experienced around the globe! Unless we fix our economy, our economy it will destroy the global economy and the domino effect will destroy the American economy; or the other way around!

When people have a lot of money, and social power, it is easy for them to buy their way into politics so that they can manipulate our economy in their favor. There is much talk about fairness today! People are concerned about economic disparity. The *quiet* elephant lurking in the room, where fairness is being discussed, is the credit monster sucking the life from the world! It is our monster; we created it and unleashed it upon ourselves!

For all you young people, who may not know credits' history, credit started out being: An arrangement by which a buyer can take possession of something now and pay for it later over time. Simple enough right. It was an agreement between the buyer and seller who often shook hands to seal their deal.

In the beginning there was also simple interest attached to long term loans. It was called simple interest because it was simple to understand. The lender would receive fair interest compensation for lending money to people wanting to buy things they could not pay for all at once. Credit made banks rich and financiers wealthy. It created a strong middle class while American jobs provided the foundation for Americans to pursue the American Dream.

Then some smart banker figured out how to steal that dream. Since it was considered USERY to charge interest rates above 10% banks and finance companies came up with a little change that would have a devastating effect upon our economy. LOAN AMORTIZATION!

The following is a simple comparison of two of the METHODS of credit manipulation we have used in our FAILED acquisition based economic system. The first financial attack on credit fairness against the middle class happened many years ago when banks decided that "SIMPLE INTEREST" was not making them enough money. Banks conspired to MANIIPULATE principle and interest payments to increase the amount of money paid to them for simply extending our payments on big ticket items. This simple manipulation changed a $10,000 dollar home loan in 1920 at 7% interest from a total repayment of $10,700 over 20 years, to a $10,000 dollar loan today with a amortized repayment of $17,214.33, which is $7,214.33 dollars in interest for the same $10,000 dollar loan at the same 7% interest!

Principle and interest loan payments, trough amortization have been manipulated so that a $20,000.00 loan with a payment of $179.77 a month only lowers the OUTSTANDING loan valance from $20,000 to 9,936.90; a mere difference of $63.10; and not to the $19,820.23 as it does on my calculator! The banking system manipulated away simple interest, replaced it with loan amortization, and turned multi-millionaires into multibillionaires. If allowed to operate unchecked, banks will subjugate all of humanity! The simple change from simple interest to amortized interest mad greed bankings' legacy to our economic existence!

$20,000 loan @ 7% INTEREST 240 payments @$88.16 a month

(simple interest) balance after a payment= $19,911.84

$20,000 loan @ 7% INTEREST 240 payments @$179.77 a month

(amortization) balance after a payment= $19,936.90

Where did the $25.48 go?

So if you want to begin to reduce the growing economic disparity between the rich and the poor; and give everyone the ability to actually pay off their loans and have money left over to put their kids through college, we need to deal with the credit monster we have created. We may even be able to reduce the rolls of the working and non working poor with fairer credit. The greedy businessmen who infest our government as greedy politicians must be replaced by people who are more mainstream. By sending people with ideas to Washington; instead of those with money, America will once again be governed by the people and for the people.

The economic quandary we have created cannot be fixed with the same kinds of greedy manipulations and happenstance that has gotten us here. Happenstance and manipulation are failed tactics that have been used by a succession of visionless leaders; who have combined to create a failed economic system that fails to address any of the intrinsic economic problems we have created, or encountered, with our archaic system of acquisition. The recent enthusiasm of some of the wealthiest Americans to give more of their money away is a testimony to the strength of the morality and common decency that is in most of us. I am sure that many of our generous philanthropist are sincere in their efforts to ease the pain and suffering of their fellow men; but I also wonder how any of them (the super rich), will feel about the changes, proposed herein, that will forever end the need for their philanthropy.

Institutionalized charity should be a humiliation for any successful civilization. Charity helps the poor stay poor and makes the rich feel they are being magnanimous by shouldering the enormous burden of their fellow men. The spirit of charity is well intentioned, but the cost of institutionalizing charity is social mediocrity. Our failure can be measured in the millions of meals eaten without dignity, and in the number of millions of people who lack adequate shelter, clothing, healthcare, educations, and those who need help with basic human survival. The perpetual need for institutionalized charity is a human travesty. The only way to end the *need* for charity is for us to evolve economically to a system of value and productivity based distribution; where all basic survival infrastructures are a birthright.

We cannot recover from the billions of dollars worth of destruction caused by the worlds' natural disasters with charitable donations! The only true social safety net is a value and distribution based economic system. Haiti, India, Japan, The Philippines, every other country in the world, and many places in America, have been, and will be struck, time and time again by natural disasters. Many hard hit places have never recovered and continue to struggle with rebuilding their lives. We need to start thinking about building new self contained cities to relocate the billions of people affected by catastrophic disasters who cannot return home. And we must build cities to prepare for the billions who are facing rising sea levels. We need to repair and expand infrastructure around the world and there is no way to accomplish these goals with a social economic system that depends on tax dollars. To end the need for taxes we need to evolve economically.

Now that I have satisfied my own questions about how a cashless, tax less economic paradigm would work and how to get there, from here; I am ready to share this paradigm with a world desperately seeking long term economic answers. For the career politicians who will oppose this radical change I can only ask that they examine the: Proposed Amendment to the Constitution of the United States of America to Establish Economic Rights, at the end of this book; playing close attention to the closing sentence.

A successful society must exist on the strength of the individuals who participate in it. And each individual must be able to stand on their own two feet while they do. Like those on the far right I am for less government and paying NO taxes. Unlike them I believe that the problem with government is not its' size but its' inefficiency and over-manipulation. We can end taxation *while* ending the need for charity, ending poverty, providing free healthcare, and free education; while still providing a vital social safety net for when disasters strike.

Like the far left I also believe that collective bargaining is a vital right that was needed to insure that companies pay honest wages and provide tangible benefits to their employees. Unlike them I believe that the company should have the last say about modernization and resource usage over any union. I believe in the formulas put forth in this book that regulate executive compensation and tie executive compensation directly to the amount of productivity the executives are responsible for. It is a fair and equitable paradigm that secures an executives' ability to obtain, and maintain, lifestyles of opulence based upon their position in the company and how much human productivity they are responsible for. That's right! Your products, services, and the number of people working for you will all help determine what your executive compensation is. Lay off people... lose money! We need to forever end the practice of gutting the workforce for profit!

This book may not be for you if you are singularly satisfied and do not feel that we must do whatever is necessary to perpetuate the existence of the human race. If you are singularly satisfied and see the plight of hungry children down the street from you, as being their own fault, or when you see starving children on your television, and it does not move you; then this book may not be for you. If you are incapable of, or tend to ignore common sense reasoning, thinking outside the box, exploring new ideas, or if you blame *people* for their inability to work, satisfy their hunger, clothe themselves, shelter themselves, or educate themselves, then this book is not for you. Even though it is you who need it the most.

The gap between rich and poor is widening because of the disastrous political policies and the amoral practices of greedy businessmen who also have control of our government when they become politicians. If I talked about all of the malicious manipulations of our economic system, that have brought us down, it would take longer then I have left to live. The time it took for me to turn my dreams into paradigms was long enough. I read a lot about modern economics and couldn't find a clear path that would save humanity from the manipulations we've made to our acquisition based economic systems.

Something has to be done, fast, to bring economic relief and economic stability to the people of the world; something concrete that will allow us to repair and expand our infrastructure so the we can perpetuate the human existence, economically, socially, and morally until we meet our natural end! Because I know that I live in the most dangerous nation in the world for the introduction and propagation of new ideas, I realize that I will offend enough of the demigods, criminals, and economic predators in the world, with the resources and impudence to buy lives, that I may not have time to publish a second!

The people who wield all the power and money in this world, and prey off the masses, will want to silence my voice when the full impact of my message reaches them! With this book I know that I am planting the seeds of change and/or the seeds of revolution. I hope that this book will blossom into dialogue, and eventually into laws that bring about real, positive, social-economic change, relief, and stability to the people of the world. I hope the paradigm, I put before you in this book, will survive to be used when civilization is at the precipice of economic extinction. I hope the paradigms I've created survive me and are used to save my children, grandchildren, and the rest of mankind from lifetimes of economic struggle and uncertainty.

Social engineering is a necessity if we are to be successful as a species. Social engineering is our obligation if we are to leave our children and grandchildren the trillions of dollars of debt we will leave behind. Social engineering must be positive for all involved and I believe that I have managed to satisfy the driven, who amass great fortunes, while leveling the playing field for those, who are now labeled "dependent" and give everyone a path to achieve self reliance. We must first realize, as a global community, that our existing system of acquisition has failed. It has failed because of the economic disparity it has created. It has failed because it RELIES of the institutions of charity to continually save humanity. We must understand that before we can pick up and move on to a *value based system of distribution* that will address ALL of our social needs. And I want wealthy people to feel that the system has worked for them and not be made to feel that their success adds to the poverty of others.

Lastly, we must overcome the illusion that we are **OWNERS of ANY-THING** and accept the **FACT** that we are, and can only be, **PRODUCERS AND USERS** of the fruits of our labors. The illusion of owning personal property, cars, boats, planes, and things we use during our lifetime is just that, an illusion. We can purchase things we are able to use; but we all know, from early in the game, that we can't take it with us.

The businesses we build, or run and the political offices we aspire to are all fleeting. It is time for us to face the reality that we are just passing through this life. During our time here we should aspire to be good to each other and to being good tenders of the resources of this earth.

I've written and spoken to hundreds of people who can't seem to wrap their heads around the concept of a cashless economic system. If you read on you are not one of them. The reason some people don't even want to get this paradigm is that they have an agenda that requires the ambiguity of cash. Everything we do, of a criminal nature, requires the use of an ambiguous medium of exchange to carry it out; and that means cash. **No** cash is the answer to our problems. Having cash is the object of our dreams. Both of these are powerful opposing forces that we must choose between.

Chapter 2

A PIECE OF MY MIND

As I write this book I know that for my ideas to be accepted by a majority of the worlds' people, they must offer strong arguments to change the worlds opinion of the physical currency we use. My arguments can offer no less than answers to solve our intrinsic economic problems forever. Everyone is standing in line for a chance to manipulate this economy through political change that supports their social-economic agendas. It will take a strong argument to convince the left, right, and centered Americans that evolving, economically, into a value and distribution based economic system is the right thing to do. I submit that due to the biblical sized failure of our acquisition based economic system, evolving is the only thing we can do if we are to extricate ourselves from an ever looming global economic collapse.

If I was the richest man in the world, the month I die I would still get an electric bill, water bill, phone bill, and have monthly obligations. I couldn't, say, call the phone company and pay for phone service forever. I wouldn't pay my employees off! If I was the richest man in the world I could not live free of debt! Our economic system didn't go far enough. It is not secure enough. It is not manipulation proof or theft proof, and will always fail the needs of the individual and humanity as a whole.

Regardless of your own singular economic satisfaction we must address the growing economic need in the world that is costing trillions of dollars and millions of lives. I hope to help you reach an understanding of the economic remedy being presented before the naysayers decide that our system of acquisition is sacrosanct. It is something that many will not want to try. If naysayers had their way, we could not fly or transplant hearts. We never would have made a choice about employing the failed acquisition based economic system we currently employ. We were raised with it, and if not enough of us can see what is outside the box, it will lead to our end. If you presented me with another choice that had no problems, no need for constant manipulation, was fair and rational I would listen and possibly even choose it. I welcome any debate of ideologies. My goal here is to explain a different choice, keep it simple so that anyone choosing to read this book can fully understand the economic paradigm I will put before you in this book.

There will be some natural fear. It will dissipate when you see the benefits that these changes will bring. There will be strong opposition to any new economic paradigm that produces radical change. That is why I challenge anyone to openly debate with me. Most of the natural opposition will come from people who are criminally committed to possessing and using physical currency as an ambiguous medium of exchange for their criminal activities. They will summarily dismiss any alternative that excludes the use of physical currency, because monies ambiguity is critical to their economic viability. Politicians who sell their votes will no longer be able to sell us out. But no matter what the social benefits are there will still be people who will continue to stand in opposition to an economic system based on fairness and positive social engineering. Even if it eliminates all international, national, and personal debt, ends our governments' need for taxes, ends the need for millions of economic based charities, and ends needless economic suffering around the world.

It is a system that will allow us to pick up and rebuild lives and critical infrastructures after natural or unnatural disasters. It is a system that allows doctors, nurses, and millions of technicians and healthcare workers to heal and care for us as the need arises. It is a system that allows teachers, our police, our military, and our governments to contribute their services and share the products and services provided by the rest of us. It is a system that insures people will not freeze or die of heat because they had no access to energy; and it is a system where everyone eats with dignity, is sheltered, and has access to free education at every level. It is a world worthy of the children of God.

The use of misinformation by the worlds' economic aristocracy, has rendered the worlds' governments ineffectual, protected the greedy, and plunged the world into an economic abyss called debt. A totally new, radical, out of the box, yet simple, economic idea that solves all of our problems, has to be prepared to cut through any campaign of misinformation that will surely be launched against it. The plan I lay before you, others will attempt to demonize because of their own need for an ambiguous medium of exchange. You, the readers who understands, must carry the real message to those unfortunates who are unable to or unwilling to read it for themselves. I am trying to save the world. In order for a new idea to gain the acceptance of the majority of the people of the world, it must be clear enough to help all of us envision the same goal. It is my sincerest hope and belief that the clarity and simplicity of the ideas presented in this book will make it possible for us to achieve the lofty goals in it. And I hope these goals will serve as a platform to promote global economic relief and stability. We need to plan and establish a new global economic system.

Our day to day economic environment is critical to our ability to sustain global life. An economic environment should be as natural as nature. Our current acquisition based economic system has failed to meet the basic survival needs of our global civilization without using trillions of dollars in global economic aid. It is expecting a great deal of any book to unite the world in a global evolution revolution. This writers' challenge is to propagate a positive message that should be found acceptable to the worlds' governments, big business leaders, small business owners, doctors, technicians, factory workers, farmers, teachers, fast food workers, religions communities, the rich and the poor. I hope a productivity driven, value and distribution based economic system will unite us all in a single pursuit that will redefine the meaning of humanity!

In the world of science fiction the people of the world always come together when faced with global annihilation from an outside force or threat. Aliens, asteroids, strange diseases, or Mother Nature, we fight them all in order to maintain human life as we know it. This book targets the elephant in the room that is our crumbling global economy. This book has no other agenda than to bring economic relief and stability to the people of the world. With it I hope to perpetuate the human economic existence by laying a blueprint for our economic success in that oh so important life class I call "Living 101".

In these days of growing global natural and manmade environmental disasters it is imperative that we construct an economy that is capable of helping people recover when they have lost everything; without the need for raising billions of charitable dollars. Insurance can never compete with economic rights that can focus available resources on restoring peoples' lives after surviving a natural, or unnatural, disaster requiring a multi-billion dollar economic response.

It will be hard for many people to accept the concept of a working, stable distribution based global economy. The boogieman, some call socialism, will take on new meaning in the value and distribution based economic system propagated here. Those who fear a *social* economy will be putting up a smoke screen if they cry "socialism" as practiced in an acquisition based economy. The need to distribute and use physical currency made "socialism" a heartbreaking pipe dream. The economic ideology here creates a fair, cashless economy that is new and fresh, and I can only hope that it will be accepted as such. While a cashless economic system may not be a unique concept, the paradigm, and philosophy behind this one is unique.

Our distribution based economic system *is* a social economy; in that it encompasses the whole of our global society. However, it is driven by the important qualities of free enterprise, quality, craftsmanship, and productivity; coupled with the important human qualities which are personal drive and ambition. That it can all be done without physical currency, is what makes it unique.

Some people will fear that this new economic system will take away their ability to reach the financial goal of opulence. Indeed, opulence will still be an obtainable goal but it will ONLY come from the creation of productivity outlets (jobs), instead of graft and greed. Our proposed changes will revive ethics and thwart the strong moral weaknesses that have entrenched corruption and greed in the power centers of businesses and governments around the world. Only hard work will bring about opulence and no one will be able to make their wealth off of the unfairly exploited labors of others.

The perpetual political power struggles, that distract our *leaders* from their true purpose, will only end when we establish an economic system that only needs tending to and is not in a constant state of economic turmoil and manipulation. We are mired in an economic quagmire from which there is no escape through business manipulations, government manipulations, regulations, deregulations, or through our protracted political squabbling. Our only real economic escape will come when we establish permanent, evolutionary, and global economic changes that allow us, as a global community, to master *Living 101*.

The billions of poor people around the world, who only pass what little money they get around anyway, will still see the end of monies use as an end to their dreams of having it; so that they can access a new lifestyle for themselves and their families. They dream of fulfilling their personal whimsical dreams of possessing things of value, and yes, they even dream of fulfilling their illegal and immoral desires. They will be able to realize their dreams! Our social, government, and economic systems must be stronger then our collective, and individual, greed and moral weaknesses. Through the use of modern technology only illegal activities require an ambiguous medium of exchange in order for the transactions to take place. Physical currency is the ambiguous medium of exchange needed to corrupt and bribe officials and it is the only medium that makes crime profitable. With plastic access cards there will always be a paper trail. No more secret monetary transactions, and no more anonymous transactions that buy peoples' lives. Oh sure, you can, if you are wealthy enough, change the lives of anyone you wish. You can have your bank issue them an access card that will forever enhance that person's life. But there will be a paper trail back to you.

I fear that the fruition of the ideas put forth in this book will never be obtained because of the *power* that physical currency has over the human mind. Physical currency has led to the moral and physical degradation of our global society; and the problems created by physical currency cannot be fixed with physical currency. Although I am not a fatalist, I just don't believe that we, as a people, are capable of unilaterally doing what is right. That being the case I, for the P.O.W.E.R.S organization, have submitted, in the appendix of this book, a Proposed Amendment to the Constitution of the United States of America to Establish Economic Rights, which, if made law, will establish rights to the critical infrastructures of: housing, sustenance, education, healthcare, and energy, for every US citizen. It is an instrument, which will help us to mold our communities, cities, and country into the dream our founders envisioned, and we still pursue. Because it offers "0" potential for undetectable corruption or manipulation, it can help us repair the moral fabric of our society by establishing, for us, an economic system worthy of the children of God.

Our global fascination with physical currency terrifies me! Equally terrifying are our quest for power and feelings of superiority we have over others. Money makes some people feel that they are better than others. An erroneous feeling many take to their graves. Money and power are strong catalyst that drive business and government corruption. The same forces that drive us to become successful are also responsible for the moral deficit of our citizens. Our voices for change have fallen upon many deaf ears during P.O.W.E.R.S. struggle because we offer only economic relief and stability for the people of the world; as our catalyst for change. Change will likely only come through conflict because far too many of us are only motivated by personal gain. No matter what benefits our economic changes may bring to the rich and the masses, some people will find it hard to except any paradigm that does not include the hoarding, manipulation, and economic dependence upon physical currency. We have to think outside the box of our current economic boundaries, and limitations, if we are to break our addiction to power, greed, and partisan political manipulations promoted by the quest for money. We must divest ourselves of our need for physical currency if we want to survive this economic collapse; and prevent any future ones.

People Offering World Economic Relief & Stability has solved, to this writer's satisfaction, the worlds' worst and most complex economic problems with a simple, designed, evolutionary, economic methodology that does not require the use of physical currency or taxes. Getting there is simple and the transition can be accomplished with a simple pen stroke! A change to a distribution based economic system may sound like a bitter pill to some, but its positive effects will save both lives and resources.

With this book I hope to launch the greatest crusade for economic evolution ever undertaken. It is my goal to, without revolution or bloodshed, insure the economic survival of the human race. For me, any economic changes we make must be constitutionally based so that they will be permanent and free of loopholes. Any changes must be fair, and perpetual so that they will stand strong against the manipulations of individual, corporate, or political economic greed. Our *plans* to straighten out the world's economy includes many *philosophical* economic changes that addresses all of the worlds' economic problems; with only one obvious physical change. It will require us to end the use of physical currency when conducting legitimate business transactions.

The philosophical changes that will take place in an evolved economy will include positive changes in banking practices. This will come with the initialization of fair employer-employee compensation paradigms, and by changing the dynamic roles of banks, businesses, insurance companies, the IRS, and our government. These will all be clearly outlined in our proposed amendment. Our planned economic system will end taxation while it encourages local, state, and federal government spending. It addresses and conquers the critical social issues of poverty, infrastructure expansion and repair, education, crime, religion, race relationships, healthcare and energy. Because our approach was to simplify economic processes rather than complicate them, the changes P.O.W.E.R.S. envisions will be able to exist in our intense technological environment as well as in unindustrialized countries that are devoid of widespread technological infrastructure.

Our lives, at least the quality of them, are dependent upon us establishing a *system* of economics designed with the needs of mass civilization in mind! From the cradle to the grave we are all dependent upon our economy for survival. If a child is left without parents, or a person becomes disabled, for any reason, then that child, or disabled person, should have a constitutional right to a basic economic existence based upon their status as a human being; and never be labeled as a "dependent"! As a user of the proposed economic system I only asked what I would need to have economic access to legitimate markets. Then I asked what medium would be needed to track my productivity and my usage of the products and services we provide. The answer was simple... plastic access cards. As a participant in this planned economy, I wanted to make sure it would be fair, secure, and that it would not be corruptible by its' administrators or criminally motivated users. The severity of our economic situations required a solid solution that will save and enrich lives. The solutions in this book are those that we need as participants in a global economic system to make global human economic existence not only possible but perpetual as well!

What led to the economic collapse of our economy is subject matter for economist and historians to muse and write about. This book is about advancing a paradigm to launch our civilization toward an economic era that will give all people the ability to access the critical infrastructures that are necessary to sustain life. We are submitting, for your approval, the first planned economic system designed to give all people access to the American dream. The necessity for us to live inside, to eat with dignity, to get an education, to have healthcare, use energy, and have an opportunity to work and contribute to a happy, healthy, and prosperous society is the reason we need this. It is the only way for us to make use of our gift of life; and fulfill our dreams of liberty.

An individual's personal drive and ambition, establishes their earned economic compensation. This combination will continue to determine how much of the dream we have earned access to. Our individual abilities and productivity, in a value and distribution based economic system, will still enable us to have a diversity of socio-economic levels of earned economic access. None of those earned economic access levels, however, will be below the poverty level, which has created millions of working poor, while the opulence achieved by a highly productive few will not create mass poverty for the rest of the world. And, finally, we have a clear path to put a planned economic system into place quickly and efficiently. Our economic rights amendment is a blueprint on how to get us to a planned economy from where we are now. Our path had to make it possible for us to integrate our new; distribution based economic system into our failing acquisition based economic system, with as little disruption as possible to our daily lives. I was surprised to find that everything was already in place for our ECONOMIC EVOLUTION to take place! Our financial infrastructure is already fully capable of encompassing three hundred million Americans, and billions worldwide, who need a pathway to economic stability. Only the way that we use our financial infrastructure, needs to be changed!

We say that necessity is the mother of invention. Necessity has served as the catalyst for many great inventions and innovations that have changed the way that we live. We are a cleaver and capable people who have met many challenging situations with clear thoughts, workable plans, our abilities and meaningful actions! We are a people driven by success and we have come to believe that anything our minds can conceive can become a reality. We are seldom amazed by our intellectual, physical, medical, or technological capabilities. We expect that we will continue to make new discoveries and make progress in all areas of our lives. Our medical and technological capabilities are waiting for our economy to evolve so that we may take full advantage of our science, medicine, and combined technological knowledge; and put them to use improving our environment and our everyday lives! We are descendants of people who dreamed of, and learned to fly; people who dreamed of, and visited the moon; people who made a heart, put it in a body, and expected it to work and if we continue to dream we can continue to grow and evolve. We have made a lot of progress and have excelled in medicine and technology, yet we have failed to create an economic environment capable of combating greed, poverty, crime, illiteracy, and inadequate healthcare. We have failed to supply everyone with necessary use of available energy and failed to make use of better technologies. We have stretched our imaginations to contemplate surviving every threat except the economic chaos we find ourselves mired in. It is as simple as this. In order for one of us to survive economically, we must first except that it is necessary for all of us to survive, economically!

Through all the economic horrors we've created for ourselves and survived, we have still managed to somehow retain enough of our humanity that lessening the economic suffering of people throughout the world is still important to most of us. It is time for us to harness what remains of our humanity and use it to conquer the crippling grip of a failed system of acquisition that is itself the *cause* of poverty, hunger, ignorance, and the neglect of human life! The overwhelming demands for money to address the needs of a global society are the death throbs of our archaic, and dying, system of economics!

Our greatest economic problems are caused by the very real need for us to extract our livings from each other. With our hands deep into each others' pockets we have created an economic system that inspires greed, corruption, mass poverty, and political chaos. Greed is so strong, and pervasive, in our economy that we have come to except these devastating intrinsic economic problems, like taxes and poverty, as the cost of doing business. The rich getting richer and the poor getting poorer are also, tragically, accepted as normal! Our normal business practices of generating profit, interest, fees, and fines has systematically caused poverty, the global healthcare crisis, illiteracy, and crime. We must change these failed business practices in order for us to establish an economic system capable of encompassing the needs of six and a half billion people!

The credit monster we have created is the worst of our business practices. It has led to the practice of imposing criminally high interest rates on the worlds' poorest people. When we hear that interest rates are being lowered it is only for people who do not need it! Try getting the advertized 0% interest rate on an old or new car loan if you are poor. Anything over 10% interest was once considered *USURY - "The lending of money at an exorbitant rate of interest"*! It is now a common practice, and legal, to charge any interest rate you can; if you can get people desperate enough to sign on the dotted line. I have seen payday loans charge as much as 99% interest on the money they loan. Our nation is becoming a credit risk! People often choose to default on their loans once they feel they have repaid enough on these loans to cover the amount of what they borrowed plus reasonable interest. They will let you send in another credit report for the rest. Where is our governments protection of our pursuit of happiness! Where are the laws limiting interest rates and repayment amounts! Usury of the poor must stop!

Another dangerous business practice is the accumulation of astronomical wealth while pretending to be ignorant to the plight of starving children and homeless families in your own community. Wealth accumulated without insuring that enough is left to benefit the families of the employees who created it should also be a crime. People are kept poor by employers who place as low a value on their labor as they can. It should be illegal if their employees *perpetually require public assistance* while these employers sit on at the billion dollar round tables. Employees miss having any quality of life while company executives stuff the company profits into their astronomical personal bank accounts. We need laws that make it illegal to pay low wages for low wages sake. If a company makes a profit off of their unskilled laborers they should share that profit enough to keep their employees off of welfare rolls!

When regular people have economic situations they cannot overcome; such as losing a job, or dealing with a medical emergency, they are punished with bad credit reports that can keep them from finding employment or a place to stay. It is not because the poor can't pay, because they do! They pay more for rentals of things they cannot afford to buy. They pay higher car payments, and they pay higher down payments because they are considered a "credit risk". The words "credit risk" seem to be a license for economic oppression and out and out robbery of the poor! Who gave businesses the right, and the ability, to economically punish people for having wages to low to support their families? We are fast becoming a society of share croppers. Banks make millions off of the poor with high interest rates, bounced check charges, and fee after fee after fee. The poor are not an economic risk, but rather, they are fodder for the fires that make profits that turn millionaires into billionaires. The poor are economic lambs being led to the slaughterhouses of the moneylenders who make millions from their misfortunes of having low wages. Why does our government stand by and let the poor be trampled upon by employers, banks, and greedy finance corporations? What keeps poor Americans poor? The low wages employers are *allowed* to pay by our visionless and corrupt government; and the sickening profit margins that are more important to businesses then the people generating them! Not allowing people to negotiate their wages only helps to make poverty in America perpetual.

Why don't we have economic penalties for employers who pay wages so low that their employees require public assistance while their executives and owners sit at the billion dollar round table? Why don't we penalize the grocer for pricing produce so high that it rots on the shelf instead of feeding the hungry? Where has the "common sense" marketing gone that once emphasized volume sales rather than our current practice of "whatever the market will bear" pricing! And where has the public consciousness gone that should scream UNFAIR to the greedy lenders who make their fortunes off of the sweat of the under paid people who work for them. The poor are poor because they are at the mercy of the rich who think only about getting richer! Businesses don't call a customer poor. They call them "credit risk" so that they can feel justified fleecing them in the credit contract. Calling credit applicants "poor" would make us look like the greedy bastards we really are; when we gouge and loan the poor money at the highest interest rates in the history of legal finance. Interest rates above ten percent should still be considered usury by legitimate businesses. We need to make room in our prisons for employers who make millions in profits while paying wages so low that their employees require Medicaid or use emergency rooms for care, and beside them we should make room for greedy politicians who have allowed companies to make obscene profits from the economic misfortunes of others!

Why must people be penalized, economically, for seven to ten years just for having poor credit? People who break criminal laws fair better. Who made it legal for businesses to impose economic penalties anyway? And why has our government sat idly by and let business practices crush the freedoms once guaranteed by our constitution. Credit has morphed itself into something far too ingrained and influential in our lives. Credit is only supposed to allow for extended payments and is not supposed to be a roadblock for us in any way! To let a temporary circumstance cost a person a home or car he or she was paying for, is a symbol of the fragility of our aging economic system, and a condemnation of the "everyman for himself" and "dog eat dog" mentality of our people. We attempt to hide our boorish behavior behind euphemisms called "free enterprise" and "profitability" but we have stumbled into a system of economics with no safeguards for the lifestyles we are able to obtain and must now struggle to maintain. Most of us don't have a golden parachute. A missed pay check can ruin our family's lives and affect our futures. Unless our government steps in and regulates wages and interest rates for essentials like homes, cars and furniture, the American dream will continue to vanish from the minds, and realities of the American people. The loss of those dreams is giving way to global despair and anger that has historically ended in economic revolution. It is unfortunate that successful revolutions end up ushering in a different group of visionless economic manipulators who will continue to put their own survival above that of everyone else.

The worlds' leaders seem to only be capable of securing the economic futures of a handful of new aristocrats. They need to make rich people so that they can campaign and make promises. They need to enrich these aristocrats so that they can get money for their political campaigns and continue to keep themselves rulers of nations! It is the duty of our elected officials to protect every American from threats to our lives, our liberty, or our pursuit of happiness. They swear an OATH to do it! Our economy now threatens the lives, happiness, and liberty of every American; so it is important to remember that if all of us don't survive… none of us will! Our American Constitution calls for "a government for and by the people" and provides for the people to elect their leadership. Poor people must realize that they are a political power in order for things to change! They must band together in order to keep from being exploited by greedy businesses intent on exercising their influence on our governments; making our governments more fascist then democratic. "Fascism" is **any movement, ideology, or attitude that favors dictatorial government, centralized control of private enterprise, repression of all opposition, and extreme nation-**

alism. In many states governments are moving to repress any opposition. Many seeking office lean towards a dictatorial government paid for by centralized private enterprises that impose their will on the people through the politicians they control. Most of our government is being held hostage by modern day fascist who are extreme nationalist willing to throw the rest of the world under the bus!

Our prisons are exploding with growing populations as more and more people fail to meet the economic challenges of surviving in an unstable economy. Not all of the two and a half million in prison are bad people. God didn't make that much junk! As our prison population approaches three million, with no end in sight, economic forces batter our hapless middle and lower classes sending many of them to jail, into the streets, and into their graves. Our impotent leaders continue to try and manipulate our broken economy just to save their jobs and they are not trying to find permanent solutions to our global economic problems. Foreclosures, evictions, job closings, rising prices, natural disasters, social despair and government impotence will cause more and more people to hate their existence and long for a release from the struggles of life. Life, the greatest gift God gave to man. Once the desire for life has been extinguished, the actions of economically oppressed peoples will lead to an uprising unequalled since Marie Antoinette uttered those iniquitous words that demonstrated the lack of empathy that the rich have for the plight of the poor; and launched the French Revolution, "Let them eat cake!"

We applaud the efforts of our nation to combat terrorism. Let our leaders now show the same resolve to end the economic terrorism aimed at the poor people of this nation. Economic terrorism that can only be combated by defeating corporate greed and the political indifference that feeds and allows it. We must stop the feeding frenzy of high interest rates and unfair business sanctions that are imposed on people who can least afford them. People already beset by the pressures of existing in a fragile and uncertain economy do not need the added pressure of usury fines and interest rates. The proposed amendment at the rear of this book is intended to right the economic iniquities that are steadily growing in this country. It will bring economic relief and stability to our crumbling economy and restore hope to the masses it is currently failing.

Embedded in P.O.W.E.R.S. proposed system of economics is a formula that creates fair wages for employees while still allowing business owners to obtain and maintain their lifestyles of opulence. In P.O.W.E.R.S. economic system business and government leaders will "earn" their economic access based upon how much human productivity they are responsible for. This system will encourage businesses to hire more people and increase their productivity to meet the demands of more producers and users. Workers will "earn" diversified economic access to their value based lifestyles based upon their level of contribution (job) in creating their companies gross national product. This will remove the owner determined valuation of employees' wage entitlements and, in turn, improve employer – employee relationships. The owners and executives will still be able to grant additional economic entitlements such as bonuses and stocks, and will continue to control the organizational placement of employees. They will still be able to promote and fire but an established economic formula will determine the employees' fair wages.

P.O.W.E.R.S. proposed Economic Rights amendment will establish:

a. A society free of debt

b. A society free of homelessness

c. A society free of hunger

d. A society free of crime and drugs

e. A healthy society.

f. An educated society

g. And a poverty free society.

It is *too* easy, and utterly useless, to sit around and criticize the job performance of the worlds' visionless leaders. We all see the chaotic evidence of their failures. Over half of the worlds' people do not participate in any economic systems at all. They are dependent on crime and the direct support and charity of the half of the people in the world who are working.

P.O.W.E.R.S. has solid plans for dealing with our social economic problems. Our best answer is **P.O.W.E.R.S. Proposed Economic Rights Amendment** which can be used as a tool to bring about permanent economic changes for the people of America. It is an economic system that changes our economy in fundamental ways but still preserves our value system, allows for lifestyles of opulence, while eliminating debt, taxes, poverty and economically motivated crime. It is a system that can be administered and implemented without cost considerations and a system that could easily spread to the rest of the world. The proposed amendment, at the end of this book, offers a pen stroke solution to 98% of our economic problems. It provides for the perpetual economic existence of the American people, from the cradle to the grave, with economic rights. It is simplicity in practice and in definition. School children, college professors, and even Presidents and Congressmen can easily understand it. It will be attractive to corporate executives and to the laborers who work for them. It is a fair and equitable economic paradigm that only poses a threat to people who rely on the ambiguity of physical currency to thrive from their criminal activities and unethical behavior. A cashless economy will stop a drug deal in its tracks! It will prevent the buying and selling of drugs at the street level and it will prevent the buying and selling of sex (except in places where it is a legal activity). It may also help control some of the other moral demons that threaten our civilization!

To show P.O.W.E.R.S. unprofitable agenda there is a second offering, in the appendix of this book. It is a business plan for banks, corporations, and workers that I call LifeStyles. LifeStyles Family, Business, and Government can be used to introduce most of the economic changes propagated in this book. Within the framework of our existing, although failing, economy, we could inject some philosophical changes that would provide a safety net for people and businesses and allow government spending without taxation. I hope that governments, banks, businesses and the people reading this book will see LifeStyles as a way to end economic dependency and chaos and make better producers and users of the people who are now considered society's economic burdens. We would have to change the actual role of banks and make them the primary system of checks and balances. Credit would be reformed so that it is not an industry, only a tool. Then let America offer economic reforms, economic relief, and economic stability, along with the democracy we propagate around the world.

Allow me to share with you our positive outlook on the impact that P.O.W.E.R.S. economy will have on our society. The following chapters

contain P.O.W.E.R.S. arguments for the need, and adoption, of the evolutionary economic changes that we propose. The numbers of working poor,
staggering number of welfare recipients and the millions in need of charity
are pushing the worlds' economies to the precipice of failure! While the
shifts in the stock market affect only a few of us; its' failure will affect us
all. A few people, betting on everything from crop failures to the success of
new technologies, has proven to be too risky as it exist today. They *play* in
the stock market while the condition of humanity is steadily deteriorating
from their greed and usury of others! Can we really see economic growth in
the stock market as beneficial when the economic chaos in our communities
threatens human existence? Before I begin my organization's arguments for
change let's look at this authors, *layman's*, analogy of how our economy is
spiraling out of control.

With this I conclude my ranting. I will now, if you allow me, walk you
down an evolutionary path to a economic system capable of sustaining all
human life; to the best of our abilities. And if I choose to run for political office, I will seek the highest office in the land, in order to get a dialog
started that will bring about positive global economic reforms. I will run
a political campaign free of commercial advertizing using only the legitimate media to propagate my agenda and rebuttals. I will prove that you do
not need millions of dollars to smear an opponent if you have an agenda for
change! Thank you for continuing to read.

Chapter 3

THE SPIRAL EFFECT

What went wrong with the economic paradigm and ideology that once drove the economy of our great nation? Besides the obvious ones of greed and corruption, I have identified something else that is inbred, sinister and I see it as the primary cause of our economic collapse. This sinister force is what I call the *"Spiral Effect"*. What is the spiral effect? Think of it as an upside down hurricane with the biggest part on the bottom. Let's examine it in an imaginary macroeconomics tale that I use to explain how "free enterprise", uncontrolled greed, and the need for profit, has affected our economy and sustained the economic instability we have perpetually faced as a civilization. The spiral effect is what killed acquisition based economic systems.

The spiral effect is simple in principle, but devastating in its effect on our economy! Let's begin by mentally grouping all *like* industries together for the purposes of the manufacturing and distribution of their respective manufactured goods! Now let's give every industry a single owner. We'll say that you own all of the transportation related industries in the country. You are the sole proprietor, and employer, of millions of employees who manufacture and sell everything that moves. Now let's say that I control all of the housing related industries in the country from building them to sales. Now let's say that your brother owns all of the food industry from farms to grocery stores in the country; while my sister controls all of the utility companies from oil to coal and nuclear. Now imagine that all other industries are grouped under the individual ownership of people you know and then we can let the *spiral effect* scenario begin.

Let's begin with your transportation industry making and introducing a new car. It also happens to be the greatest car ever made and you know that everyone will want one. Because you know that your companies can make a lot of money off of this new car you decide to reward yourself, and your employees with newer, bigger, and better homes. You raise the price of your new car to help pay for those new homes, and also keep your profit margin where it is.

Now your brother, who owns the farms and grocery stores, sees your new car and decides that he wants one for himself and his employees. The second thing he notices is the increased price of the new car. No problem, he thinks to himself, he'll just add a few dollars to the price of his groceries so that he can afford the new car and keep his profit margin where it is. He then buys your new car for himself, and all of his employees.

Now along comes my sister, who controls all of our utilities. She sees your new car and decides that she wants one, and wants her employees to have one too! She notices that the price of the car and price of groceries have also increased. "No problem," she says, "I'll just increase the price of my utilities by a few dollars so that I can afford the new car, the higher grocery prices, and keep my profit margin where they are!"

Now I see your new car and decide that I want one for me and all of my employees in the housing industry. I've also noticed the increased price of the new car, the increased price of your brother's groceries, and the increased cost of my sister's utilities, so I decide to increase the cost of my houses too. This is how the spiral works to destroy us! Because we must extract our livings from each others' pockets we will continue to escalate our prices in a feeble attempt to end up with the most **profit**!

Now the workers in all of these industries also get caught up in this #@%*# spiral process. They will make up the largest portion of the spiral... the bottom portion. The auto dealership owner now realizes that he may have made the car to good. Projected new car sales start to decline! The owner decides to lay off a hundred thousand workers in order to maintain the companies' **profitability**. He also increases the price of future car sales because since the car's introduction grocery, utility, and housing cost have also increased.

The grocer follows suit, with layoff, because he must adjust for the increased cost of utilities, housing and automobiles. Eventually you will have hundreds of thousands of people not working and not able to afford the cars, utilities, housing, or groceries they used to produce. So everyone again increases their prices so that they can survive in an economy with a vastly depleted customer base that *they* created with layoffs and price increases.

They all have the same goal and necessity, to get more money from the people who are still able to buy their products in order to keep up their profitability in spite of increased mortgage rates, higher automotive cost, higher utility cost, and higher grocery cost in a market with millions now unemployed. As prices become higher, more and more people are unable to afford their groceries, mortgages, utilities and automobiles so prices continue to spiral upwards leaving more and more people unable to pay! Whatever happened to our philosophy of volume selling? Sell it all at a fair price and make a fair profit. Better to make a dollar profit from a million people rather than to try and make a million dollars in profit off of half as many people!

We can stop the spiral effect and correct the devastating effects that it has had on our civilization! The first thing we have to do is put **profitability** in perspective! As long as corporations are able to earn enough to pay their cost and restock, excess profits are really bad for our economy. They say that companies are afraid to hire. Then they don't understand the basic business principle that increases in labor forces create increases in demand for products and services. If they don't start hiring soon, all their profits will disappear anyway when there are no customers left to buy the goods being produced.

In a P.O.W.E.R.S. economy cost barriers will be removed and companies can again hire enough people to end unemployment. Quality will once again determine customer use and product sales. Increased product demand will lead to the hiring of third shifts instead of the trend now to work one or two shifts to death with overtime in order to maintain productivity and profit levels.

Next we need to stop NAFTA and CAFTA as they are currently practiced. By allowing American companies to outsource American jobs we have decimated our own employment rolls. You may be able to hire a million cheep foreigners to manufacture your products and man your call centers, but you need millions of local Americans to buy your goods. American companies that moved abroad to pay pennies instead of dollars did nothing to improve the lives of the foreign workers they employed so they did not create demand it those countries and had to export nearly 100% of the finished product back to America for consumption. It was utter stupidity for our government to allow outsourcing to decimate the American workforce. NAFTA and CAFTA should have been used to create foreign markets where American manufacturing could expand their consumer base into foreign markets, instead of them having to export consumables back to America because their foreign workers could not afford to buy them with the wages they are paid.

More people working will mean more people with money to buy more products. Increase demand and stabilize prices so that a gallon of milk cost the same in every store in America and we may begin to fix the problems with our economy!

Chapter 4

TALKING HEADS

People in politics, and the media, should ideally be among the most ethical and virtuous people in service to the rest of mankind. Our media and political processes have been heavily corrupted because of money's influence on the way the media disseminates information, and the influence that money has had over our political process is frightening! Long ago politicians stood atop soap boxes and espoused their agendas and made their promises to people. They cared about being liked and the popular vote usually reflected who the winner was in an election. Word of mouth and the fifth estate, were used to convinced voters about whom they should vote for. But the manipulation of truth by media owner's has rendered the fifth estate mute and corrupted the political process.

Media should have the integrity not to print what they know is a lie! The political ads we are seeing now and the spins being touted as truth are proof that money can corrupt anything! It amazes me that the same Republicans who benefited from the lack of participation of young democratic voters in 2010 midterm election, now fear their vote so much that they are reduced to trying to suppress the voting in 2012. Their know that their claim of a mandate in 2010 is a lie that they know will soon be exposed in the 2012 election! Media creditability has become a liability and the media is exasperating the problems of the world by not acting in the interest of the people.

Media corruption has blocked change by knowingly disseminating false information to the public. Because they are the media it leaves less examining citizens confused and misinformed about political positions and agendas. Our economy is failing and people must be informed properly in order to motivate our leadership to act so things can be changed or accomplished. Even if this book gets its' message out the changes we seek will not come easily. People will try and find a way to cheat a system before they'll be willing to change to it. If you look hard enough you may find a weakness in the design of our proposed economy, but there won't be a reason to exploit it. Modifying the economic behavior of people will take a system that negates greed and other temptations. More challenging then overcoming the allure of physical currency that people have, we have the task of getting information to people. It will take a strong system to get people to give up the desire to be corrupt, dishonest and prey on the productivity of other people. To many people physical currency has become something for them to worship. While this book may put forth some answers to help improve our struggling economy, the general lack of ethics in media, the extreme greed and political agendas of some of the owners of media outlets, are all obstructions to the dissemination of truth.

I believe that while most talking heads are basically honest, at some level, their veracity has been usurped by their greed. The lure of advertizing dollars block their integrity and sense of fairness. Our obsession with greed has pushed morality from the media and left us with news we cannot trust! Many people in the media are only soulless shells that once held reverence for truth and nurtured our sense of fair play. The media once championed honesty and spoke the truth to their fellow man. But from the tragedy in Darfur to our political discourse we are fast becoming a nation that wallows in lies, hypocrisy, greed and indifference to the truth. With the death of responsible media the future of our nation is at risk. As some in the media choose to fan the flames of intolerance, injustice; and now, dangerously, racial hatred, I see a separated nation which cannot address the problems we face if we cannot communicate truthfully. It is the media that tells the most harmful lies. Lies are destroying what has taken years to build. Lies are trying to destroy the Presidency of one of the best leaders of modern times and it is time for laws that punish inaccurate "news" reporting!

I'd hope that, by now, the seeds of change that our President has been trying to sow would have taken hold and begun to bear fruit. I hoped that we, as a people, would have started to excavate ourselves from the economic hole we were thrust into by years of bad leadership. But the influence of money in the media is strong enough to suppress the truth! Media money prevents many people from thinking outside the box of the fragile, crumbling, and archaic economy we continue to manipulate. It is a shame that some media outlets will twist and misrepresent the ideas put forth in this book; for their own economic agendas. Without even knowing the contents herein, they will try to demonize the idea that we need to change to a value, productivity, and distribution based economic system in order to progress.

If money is the root to all evil, the media is the root to shaping all social opinion. We need to rid ourselves of the media that acts as a vehicle for racism and greed while contributing to the degradation of the fifth estate. We must rid ourselves of physical currency in order to help restore media integrity. The media should not separate us and pit us against each other, for advertising money!

Where President Obama is concerned we have seen an unprecedented increase in racist media reporting. Racism is tearing this nation and economy apart and the talking heads spreading hatred and lies now have added racial tension to the backdrop of economic upheaval. Racial tension soared after President Obama's' election as did the number of white supremacist groups in America. President Obama's re-election may bring us to a tipping point of racial unrest in America. The weight of poverty is breaking the back of our economy and our society will suffer greatly if *all* of the media does not start reporting honestly to the American people! Older right wing media audiences of bigots and race haters will soon die out and organizations like FOX News will have to stop being a disgrace to free speech if they wish to develop an American audience. History will wonder why some of them were not shut down for the good of the public! I am for free speech and it will take the enlightenment of their audience to make them go away. Until then I would like to make a personal appeal to all right wing media to stop slanting the truth, news, and stop lying to people who are loyal viewers and need to hear the truth.

No "talking head" I've contacted has even responded to my overtures to start a conversation about economic evolution!. It is a discussion we desperately need to have. I also know that "talking heads" are not free to discuss whatever they to want on their news programs. Media ownership still has the last word about what gets covered! The free press that once existed in America is vanishing and the internet is still in its infancy in vetting and disseminating the news.

Chapter 5

MAN-KIND OR NOT-SO-KIND

Mankind, the brotherhood of man! Created in the image of God! Even if you don't believe in a creator, you have to acknowledge that we are *all* one basic species that we call mankind! Although we are only one species we have created, and used, many labels to describe, group, isolate and divide ourselves. We have racial labels that group us and divide us by our color, heritage, religion and nationality. We have religious and social labels that further group us and divide us into political and religious groups that further separate and divide us by our beliefs and our special interest. We have social groups that further group us and divide us by our ideologies, social associations, and professional associations. And isn't it ironic that we cannot group ourselves, without dividing ourselves from others at the same time? We have grouped and divided ourselves until we eventually stand alone as individuals and no longer even acknowledge our basic, hard wired, connections to each other. Basically, I think, there are really only two kinds of people in this world, those who care about each other, and those who don't! Mankind, or not so kind, is not hard to define!

We have created a society that we, ourselves, have labeled "dog eat dog" and "the rat race". Our politics, businesses, and even some of our religions focus on the "bottom line" rather than the people who are involved in creating it. Our economy has further divided us and isolated us from one another through the diversity between wealth and poverty. It is time that we address our human condition and our human needs, so we can rise above our many differences to become mankind!

Are we truly a brotherhood of man? Or are we individuals in a "dog eat dog rat race"? Is it too much of a challenge for us to love and live together, caringly? Are we so self-absorbed with money that we can no longer identify with each other as brothers from different mothers? Maybe if we can eliminate the economic barriers that create poverty then we can concentrate on ungrouping and un-dividing ourselves. To create a world free of a "dog eat dog" mentality, we must be able to look at each other and see someone whom we care about and respect. Then we will have accomplished something truly great! Something truly worthy of the children of God!

Many wealthy people seem to no longer feel connected to the rest of us. Their wealth has them living under the delusion that they are somehow better or smarter than the rest of us. Mankind has faced and will face, many more challenges and threats to our existence. We can do without threats from each other. Whether these threats come from nature or man, we must act together to weather the storms and rebuild our homes, communities, and restore our lives to normalcy, whenever it is necessary. We have all known of communities, towns, and cities that, after being flooded, destroyed by quakes or ravaged by fires, took the caring and labor of millions to rebuild. "There but for the grace of God go I" has been the rallying cry of those committed to helping those affected by tragedy. After the first responders do all they can to save lives it is up to the community of mankind to come together to restore human lives to their former or a better existence. Rebuilding homes, roads, schools, hospitals, businesses and places of worship cannot have a price tag. Whatever is necessary to sustain human life is just necessary! When insurance companies deny claims based on the fact that paying them would bankrupt the insurance company; it is easy to see that the only real insurance is the insurance in knowing that each individual is part of a *whole* civilization.

As the 2012 election approaches there are two distinct political sides in opposition over social issues that are all tied to the economy. One would promote human life in the womb and abandon it once it is born. The other would allow a mother to choose if a fetus lives or dies in the womb but does everything it can do to preserve, nurture and fulfill that life once a child is born. In a society where that child has a constitutional right to an economic existence mothers will be more likely to bring their children into the world; thus ending financially motivated abortions forever. Both sides win in a distribution based economic system.

The choice of whether or not to care for each other is a moral imperative that either has been instilled in us from birth or it hasn't. Where it has been we see the kindness and compassion that links us as a nation and as citizens of the world. Where it has not can be seen in people who have been raised to feel that people are a cost factor, that the needy are a drain on our resources, and while they don't understand that the excessive resources of a few is all that is keeping many people from being able to live.

The choice to abandon the poor to their own devices is a choice that will doom this attempt at building a civilization. We must remove the burden of poor people from the taxes of the rich so that they can be happy and content. The survival of humanity cannot be left to the charitable whims of the very same people who created the poor! Poor people are the result of a much deeper underlying cause, and that cause is mostly low wages. Instead of the welfare act, signed into law by President Lyndon B. Johnston, we should have passed a fair wage law. Then things would be different. All he had to do was make it illegal to pay wages so low that your employees required public assistance. An honest day's pay for an honest day's work. Low wages are the quiet elephant in the room that created the need for a public safety net. With fair wages we would have a larger tax base and would not need to channel money to the working poor with Earned Income Credit in the tax code. America is burdened by working poor who have not seen any appreciable increase in income in twenty years; and are now seeing it drop.

Mans' inhumanity to man began with unfair wages and is destined to end with the social upheavals we are experiencing across the world today. Man's inhumanity has been around a long time and is best expressed in the lines of my favorite quote:

It is eloquently stated by *Ambrose*, the magnificent fourth-century bishop of Milan, who thundered:

"Think you, that you commit no injustice by keeping to yourself alone what would be the means of life to many. It is the bread of the hungry you cling to; it is the clothing of the naked you lock up; the money you bury is the redemption of the poor."

Chapter 6

THE TROUBLE WITH MONEY

Physical Currency! What started as a simple means to an end, has become a tyrannical demigod that rules over us with cold ambiguity, moral impunity, and a total disregard for the well being of the individual, or mankind as a whole? It is the cruel task-master of our lives, and the collector of many of our souls. Money, the lack of money, the misuse of money and the ambiguity of money have caused every grief known to man. Money, the lack of it, and its' greedy influence, has turned a mother against her child, a husband against his wife, a stranger against a stranger and nations against nations. Money is the common thread contributing to every social economic dilemma and almost every domestic one. Money has woven its way into the fabric of our lives and our economic foundation and is choking us from within. Even when we agree that money is necessary to rid ourselves of some pressing social dilemmas, we are unable to focus enough money on the problem to rid ourselves of it! We've spent trillions of dollars on welfare and only succeeded in making it perpetual. We haven't put a dent in poverty although we've committed trillions of dollars in taxes toward that end. We operate our government in the red and lack sufficient quintiles of money to deal with oppressive global social problems! All of this demonstrates our need for change.

We must move now to develop a system of economics that works globally! A new system must be able to deal with the problems of, not only America, but the world; and provide participation for all of the people in it. The preservation of our civilization cannot be measured in dollars and cents. Whatever is necessary for the perpetuation of the human race is just *necessary*, and must be done! It is *necessary* that people live indoors and eat with dignity. Anyone have a problem with that? It is just necessary that we maintain our public infrastructures, transportation systems, public schools, and other public institutions. Our local and national governments, our military, our education and healthcare systems, need billions of dollars to operate yearly. Our foreign aid programs require billions more. Military spending is growing by billions every month and social upkeep and repairs to our infrastructure require billions of dollars more. A tax based economic system cannot support the economic commitments made by our governments and demanded by human necessity! Money is not the answer to modern economic problems… it is the cause of them!

We spend billions of dollars and create trillions of dollars of debt in order to access billions of dollars worth of our own productivity. The productivity needed to fulfill our economic needs has less value then what it cost to acquire and use what we've produced. We are drowning in debt because of this intrinsic imbalance. Meeting all of the economic needs of our non-profit entities is theoretically possible but it requires us to remove physical currency. How can you balance a budget and not fulfill the needs of the people? Where money, in an acquisition based economy, has failed to provide for us a simple value, productivity and distribution based economy is the answer we need. We can well define individual productivity. It is reflected in the pay check we receive. Our usage is established by the earned and granted economic access of our governments. By removing physical currency, humanity can succeed at housing, feeding, educating, providing healthcare for and distributing energy to all the people of the world! It is easier to grant our non-profit federal, state and local governments, hospitals, schools, and individuals in non-profit entities, "granted" economic access to the products and services produced by the rest of us; then it is to sell those products and services to them. We are producers and users! Products and services, that we produce, require different levels of economic access in order to access the value of those products and services, by us, the users! Even in our existing economic system there is no real need for physical currency. Money is the middleman that we created in order to place a value on the products we produce, and on the value of our service. A value that is ideally proportional to the amount of personal drive and ambition required to reach the different levels of access to our productivity. Money had its place when we fairly used it to give ourselves a way of accessing the results of our labors. Money gave us a way to measure our individual and group productivity and to reward ourselves for our athletic and artistic abilities. But money has spawned more problems for us then benefits.

Turned a mother against a child – what powerful force money is that it can have the impact it has on, what should be, an impregnable human bond. Our continuing and growing need for human financial assistance, business bailouts, infrastructure repair and expansions, and our global humanitarian response means that we will continue to operate at a deficit if we continue to meet these massive needs with our "tax dollars solve all" mentality. Providing appropriate economic access for everyone is just a bookkeeping chore! We are producers and users! Our economic system should operate based upon us putting our productivity into the system – and taking our access out of it!

For our economy to operate effectively we must eliminate its' loopholes and operational fragility. In order to strengthen and rebuild our global economy it is necessary to put in place a plan that strengthens the economic foundation that supports it. We must try to establish a worldwide economic system that provides shelter for, feeds, educates, heals and provides access to critical infrastructure for everyone! Unless we develop a more encompassing social economic system we will never be able to support the billions of people in the world with economic needs. Economic evolution will make it possible for us to effectively provide electricity, water, and other critical resources without cost, but respective to individual and group, needs. A system of economics that concentrates on the conservative use of its resources, rather than their acquisition, is essential to our economic survival and the stabilization of our global economy.

To overcome entrenched poverty we must achieve true harmony between mankind and our economic environment! Economic diversity must be based upon individual personal drive and ambition, personal achievements and individual and group social contributions. To balance the economic scales between the races, we must look beyond social welfare programs that do not have the ability to promote every individual's economic stability. Money, the physical currency that we use, is our one great enemy.

The thrust of the hard fought civil rights movement gained a measure of social freedom for everyone. P.O.W.E.R.S. proposed economic rights are now needed to dampen the effects of economic racism which continues undaunted. Our government and businesses are rife with greed and partiality. While it is impossible to maintain control of the forces that seek to influence our government, it is possible to gain control over the economic system they have to employ. We must be prepared to fight as hard for economic rights as we did for civil rights. The cost of failure will be measured in the needless suffering and deaths of people; the most valuable global resource of all!

Chapter 7

MAN AND CRIME

The economics of crime has burdened our society with many negative consequences. From a rise in civil crime to police racial profiling and criminal malfeasance, our justice system is overwhelmed. We won't have time to examine the growing *global* crisis of crime. The statistics on crime and punishment, in America, are both staggering and dismal. Two point three million Americans in prison, millions more on probation and parole, and a growing number in prisons that go on forever. The problem with crime is the HUMAN NEED economically motivated. Crime is driven by need and by greed. Because people can no longer live off of the land it is necessary for all of us to have access to available resources through acquisition. Buying things is the only way we can take care of our critical human needs.

The biggest contributor to crime, of course, is the growing abject poverty in the world. It is not caused by an unwillingness on the part of the millions of children, elderly people, and disenfranchised people who live without even an opportunity to work and support themselves. This population is not able to earn enough to participate in our economic system; that seem to be only a support network for banks. Millions of working people are unable to live a life above the poverty level, eat with dignity, educate themselves, use energy and have healthcare. When people find themselves without the economic resources needed to live, but with the same responsibilities that sustain them, crime is often all they have left. From murders to non-violent petty crimes we know that crime can happen to anyone of us, at any time, and in any place! You can't move away from crime, you can't anticipate it and we can't stop or even slow it down as long as economic pressures continue to corner honest people. The massive warehousing of human beings is not the answer to the problems of crime and justice. Building more prisons will only use up more economic resources, that could be used elsewhere. We will continue to perpetuate the necessity for crime unless we make permanent economic changes that address the needs of the masses!

With the rash of crimes being committed by the rich against the rich at the highest echelons of corporate America, and on the poorest Americans, it is time that we make some changes. The quest to be super rich is causing us to be witness to the final death throbs of our global economy. With the rich committing economic crime against the rich, banking and government officials committing crimes against everybody else, our numbers game has gotten out of hand. We have exposed the tip of an iceberg of loopholes and inadequacies in our tax system that are causes of the fallibility of our acquisition based economic system. We have collapsed, economically, into a cesspool of greed and corruption that is the greatest threat to humanity. People are not inherently bad, but I believe they can be driven by greed to commit all kinds of sins. If we get poor enough, and desperate enough to fall prey to the temptations of trying to make illegal money in order to survive, prison awaits us! I hate to say it but people turn to crime and drugs because society has failed them first, not the other way around.

So what is the answer to end economically motivated crime? Remove physical currency from the equation of living, by creating a distribution based economic system that meets the survival needs of billions of people! Our police forces are steadily growing and turning our nation into an armed police state. Our prisons are overflowing, yet across this nation the number of crimes that go unsolved, and un-prosecuted, have crippled our justice system and made us afraid and our laws seem impotent. As the threats of prison, or even the death penalty, appear not as strong as the pain of starvation and homelessness, we are forced to play catch and release with our most violent offenders. Until we permanently address the problems that create crime we will continue to spend billions and trillions of dollars, or whatever is necessary, to protect ourselves from the economically driven criminals we make. We'll continue to find the money for police, lawyers, judges, courts and jails to protect the rich from the criminals they make; but we can't seem to find the money that is necessary to prevent crime in the first place. By fulfilling peoples' basic human economic needs most of our crime will disappear. We spend around forty thousand dollars a year to incarcerate one person, but almost nothing to educate, feed, house and clothe them outside of prison walls.

We have turned our prisons into human torture chambers in our efforts to try and control the growing, long-term, violent prison populations. The new super max prisons are creating even greater problems for society as they dehumanize the inmates and turn their meaningless existence into a wretched one as well. So deplorable is mental isolation that some of the inmates released from a super max, would rather die during the commission of another felony then risk returning to a super max facility! Because we must sometimes sit in judgment of each other let us not forget what makes us human. To deny human interaction or mental stimulus to prisoners is more vengeance then it is punishment and we know to whom vengeance belongs!

Ninety-eight percent of our crime is economically motivated. Our overwhelming, life threatening, need for money has led to every kind of deviant behavior displayed by man. From murder to cheating on taxes money has impacted us all and molded us into the greedy, desperate, dispassionate, yet caring and charitable society that we have become!

The economic changes that P.O.W.E.R.S. proposes will make economically motivated crime a rare occurrence and crime in general an aberration rather then something to be expected. People do things for money because money is necessary to live. The fact that it is ambiguous means that no one is entitled to it, and because living demands it from those who are without it, crime is often the result. Physical currency doesn't care how you come to possess it. It doesn't care what you have to do to keep it either. It doesn't care about the hungry and homeless child living down the street from you. It doesn't care about the father needing surgery who can't afford to have it or the family left homeless after a natural disaster. The physical currency that is needed to sustain life is the reason life cannot be sustained without it!

Take away the physical currency that we use and adopt a distribution based economic system and the system will stop illegal drug deals, illegal prostitution, and many other illegal activities that depend upon the ambiguity of physical currency in order to exist. Take away physical currency and burglaries will stop because the thief won't be able to turn your television set into the cash they need to fulfill their own economic needs.

To provide for the masses, and prevent most crimes, an economic evolution has to take place in our society. The human race is far too fragile to depend upon passing money around to make life accessible and sustainable. We must evolve economically or face the same fate every previous civilization has faced because of mass poverty created by massive wealth and political indifference... REVOLUTION!

Here at home, and around the world, economic unrest is steadily growing. Crime continues undaunted, as peoples' lives are being lost in the battle for economic survival. To turn off the flow of people into our prisons, we must end the poverty that devours whole families and destroys the value of life. Physical currency *is* the route to all evil! Let's stop crime by taking away its' ambiguous medium of exchange. Let the dollars that represent our productivity stay in a database, or on a ledger somewhere, where they can do us no physical harm. Let us take it further and simply use data bases and ledgers to account for our productivity and account for our usage of what is being produced! Use economic evolution to take us to the next level of human economic existence. Physical currency has to go in order to stop criminal behavior!

Chapter 8

FIGHTING RACISM

Red, Brown, Yellow, Black, and White, they are precious in His sight. Jesus loves the little children of the world. These words were taught to me about fifty years ago as I sat in Sunday school. Being an American military brat, and proud black American, I have lived with varying degrees of racism all of my life. At 6'4" 250 lbs. I never had to deal with overt racism myself, (racist are not entirely stupid). We were also introduced to economic racism at a very early age. We were warned that the establishment could control most of us with meager wages and the simple yoke of a house and car payment. Social control IS the reason the establishment will fight hard to keep our economy acquisition based. American freedoms are routinely being denied to people based on their gender, race, and wealth.

Racial hatred is going to be the hardest social ill for us to expunge. It is taught in our homes where love nurtures and perpetuates it. It is strengthened in our segregated neighborhoods and schools where children get introduced to racial and economic separatism. Racism, and economic racism, permeate every aspect of life from education, to healthcare; from business, to government and even, sadly, to our religions. All that I can say about racism is, get over it!

Economic racism, unfortunately, is much worse, as it does not target any one particular race. All races are targets for economic racism. Economic racism is racism that was once designed to limit economic access to minorities. Now it is designed to economically gouge all races of poor people! It is corporate created racism with a deadly influence in every important part of our lives. Nothing will affect all aspects of economic racism, but we must still try to expunge some of it from our economy. We can challenge the economic racism that is entrenched in our economy like high interest rates, usury fees and punitive economic fines. By establishing productivity based formulas that fairly measure our productivity and adequately establish our economic entitlements, we can thwart most of the economic racism being perpetrated against the poor. Economic racism can be subtle and hidden within a company's pay structures; where it is supported by rules and regulations to give it legitimacy.

The most pervasive racist element of economic racism is its' ability to economically control others with threats of economic punishment imposed by companies without even giving you a trial! Credit reports!

People, who run our government and businesses, arbitrarily assess the value of the labor of others; and this has created the largest employer-employee wage disparity in our nation's history. Historically this disparity has resulted in a wealthy aristocracy, a struggling middle class and massive poverty levels. A concrete formula for fair labor value assessment will eliminate the iniquity between employers who sit at the billion dollar round table, and their employees who require public assistance or who languish in abject poverty. Our government needs to step in and control the punitive interest rates that are burdening the poor of America. These changes will also help eliminate the imbalance between the rich and poor! Interest rates levied against the poor, because they are underpaid and unable to negotiate the value of their own labor, must be regulated!

Once this country had unions, which elevated the wages of millions of workers; but many of those unions grew greedy, corrupt and lost their vision and employee they were designed to support. But without the unions workers are once again fair game for greedy employers who are only concerned with profits and not the human condition. This is the essence of economic racism. Let me be clear that we are not seeking a re-distribution of wealth to solve this problem; only a fair distribution of it.

From the lowliest laborer, to the Chairman of the board of major corporations, everyone needs a living wage! How can elected officials, and responsible employers, begin to rationalize $6.00 an hour being anywhere near a living wage! Poverty is caused by the earning disparity between employers and employees. That gap could be closed if we had laws to prevent the employer from amassing fortunes into the billions while employing a workforce that requires public assistance in order to survive. Maybe if we placed a limit on personal income, say two billion dollars, then those who reach that point would retire and allow someone else to be productive. The bottom line is, if you can make millions and billions of dollars it should be illegal for your employees to need Medicaid, section eight housing, food stamps, or any other form of public assistance!

This country has more people working and on welfare, then it can bear! Companies do the nation harm when the owners control BILLIONS OF DOLLARS in income and most of their employees cannot afford the medical benefits they offer, qualify for food stamps, public housing and Medicaid!

Here is the way to close the poverty gap! Close the gap by removing barriers to our economic infrastructure. We can easily end homelessness if no one objects to others living inside. We can end hunger if no one objects to everyone eating. We can end needless medical suffering, if no one objects to everyone being treated and we can end unemployment and spur our economy if everyone profits from everyone working. I have no problem with people who, through their personal drive and ambition, have earned the economic access necessary to achieve lifestyle of opulence and security. That is, after all, the American dream. I do have a problem with them bleeding their employees to achieve that opulence.

Economic racism is practiced by those who control the flow of physical currency in this country. Those who control physical currency demand loyalty and submission for the paycheck they sign. Physical currency is holding us back just as racism has been used to hold back oppressed social groups throughout history. If we do not stop using physical currency we will become a nation of sharecroppers who trade at the general stores of our masters. Only an economic system with a formula for employee compensation can end economic racism.

Chapter 9

MAKING EDUCATION PAY

The battles being fought, across America, to ensure that our children get a good education are 100% economically based. Getting an education is the social obligation of our children and the economic responsibility of the rest of us. First of all let me ask the question, why do we call our school system nonprofit? Is it non-profit because we feel that we derive nothing tangible and nothing of value from educating our children? Do we not see the profit in every child becoming a productive, well adjusted, contributing member of society? We've spent, and are spending, billions of dollars on building and upgrading our schools, on inadequate teacher's salaries, on astronomical administrative cost, and staggering transportation cost, every year; just to see too many of our children struggle and dropout! Add to the actual cost of running our school systems, the collateral social cost of what we pay when the school systems fail our children: courts, judges, lawyers, prisons, victims' assistance, and lifelong dependency on welfare, then you can see that our educational system needs a serious overhaul.

Perhaps if our children viewed their educational opportunity as a real job and not just a mandatory opportunity they should take advantage of, they would perform better in school. P.O.W.E.R.S. view on education is to make it profitable to the student as well as the teachers. Children have their own value system. While some parents can easily provide incentives and rewards for their child's academic performance, others must sacrifice, or are just unable to offer the same material incentives to their children.

Since going to school is the social obligation of our children, let's give them some economic incentives to spur the personal drive and ambition in them that is necessary to make them competitive; and combat the peer pressures they face. For good attendance and academic performance in school, let our children earn some economic access to the things they value, as in the cell phones, Ipods, clothing (gear), toys and other things that they value are cheaper to provide than jails, prisons, and welfare. Let our schools become a place of employment that our children look forward to attending and receiving wares for their efforts. Let their attendance afford them the healthcare, sustenance, and clothing they need, regardless of their parent's abilities to provide it for them. Let them earn their economic independence from the moment they enter school, so that as adults they will be used to standing on their own two feet. Let schools be self pace so that children who excel can move ahead of their class to the next level of courses. Let their scholastic performance, through graduation, pay for their college or trade school and let their sexual responsibility earn them their first car or world cruise. The benefits to society will be well worth the merchandise our kids purchase through their educational productivity.

Our valued teachers' lifestyles would then be based upon the academic success of their students, as well as their longevity as teachers. Teachers know what levels of economic access they can expect when they take a position in education. P.O.W.E.R.S. system of economics will reward teachers better than they are rewarded now. Our shortcoming, now is that some school systems have the ability to better compensate teachers while equally qualified teachers, in poorer school systems, suffer economic burdens in order to teach. There are many teachers who spend their own meager resources to provide the tool their students need to succeed. Relieving the financial stress and budget distractions will help our educators and students. I would take it a step further. I would give an economic incentive to students and make them feel that getting an education was their job. With "working" students the cost of education would actually decline and our kids will start competing academically again. We could then work on bullying and any other blocks to them getting a good education.

Some children may only, academically earn the right to attend trade schools while those who show the aptitude or have their parent's productivity to supplement them, will continue on to college. There will be no financial barriers to higher education! The only barriers will be a student's own personal drive and ambition.

Remember, if teachers work for a lifestyle, and not the paycheck they use to access and maintain it, then our educators will earn their livings based on their valuable contribution to our children. A home, a car, subsistence, clothing and ample economic access, free of bills, taxes, and worries, will allow a teacher to concentrate fully on teaching and allow their students to concentrate fully on learning!

Chapter 10

HELP FOR HEALTHCARE

Healthcare is an issue that is critical to all of us. Most of the people in the world are without modern healthcare, health insurance or life insurance. To build a successful civilization, we desperately need to overcome healthcare issues that leave the majority of the world vulnerable to sickness and preventable diseases! When people without insurance need medical treatment or surgery, it falls on the rest of a strong community to provide it. Still many people must choose between working and maintaining life or getting the medical treatment they need. It is often a hard choice to make. In many communities the technology and medicine is not available to allow their hospitals to give the best medical care. In America, however, we're still more fortunate than most of the world! Still millions of Americans are forced to do without medical care because their wages are not sufficient to afford medical coverage.

In many areas the compensation for medical professionals is not attractive enough to attract medical professionals to the area. Many small communities are left without a simple medical clinic. And even where the community is prosperous, some surgeries may not be offered to some people, because they can't afford it. Some of us are simply allowed to die. This from doctors who take an oath to do no harm, but are forced by administrators decisions to allow deaths to happen. In many cases if you choose the surgery when it's available you may drown yourself in debt; losing your home and all you've worked hard for. Don't take on the debt and you may still die.

With the marvels of modern technology and medicine working miracles in our hospitals every day, it is easy to see what we are capable of achieving. The cost is the only thing keeping the technology and medicine from the people of America, and the world. The suffering that could be conquered by a small pill or new technology is worth every effort to bring about change. Cost cannot be a factor in the saving of lives. We have an obligation to use the dominion we were given by God, over our lives, to do everything to preserve them. Every life is important, and from the cradle to the grave every one of them will require medical care!

Believe it or not, the healthcare problem in America is one of the easiest problems to fix. The productivity of every doctor and nurse is measurable in the good that they do caring for us. The productivity that goes into the development of medical technology and medicine is also measurable. Since productivity equals economic access, the rewards for the people who provide medical care, medical technology and medicine, can be measured in the life-styles they are able to obtain and maintain. What healthcare workers do is also a social necessity. Their economic access should be granted to them as it is measured now, by their ability, their specialty, and the personal drive and ambition it took them to reach their level of expertise. Our hospitals should be able to access all the equipment, supplies, and whatever else is necessary to perform their services and maintain their capability to protect life. Everyone benefits from a healthy society and a happy healthcare workforce!

With everyone giving a portion of their productivity to insure that they and their family has healthcare, it is a simple bookkeeping chore to provide quality economic access for our medical practitioners and hospitals. Once we allow our economic access to be based upon our established level of productivity, bookkeeping is all we need to provide lifestyles for doctors, nurses, and the medical technicians who treat us. Life insurance is a tool we use to provide for those who survive us. We set aside some of our accu-mulated access from our productivity every week to insure that the lifestyle we have given our family can be maintained in the event of our death. Even though every individual has a right to economic access, insurance is intended to maintain the quality of our family's life! From birth to death our membership in humanity should afford us sustenance, shelter, clothing, educations and anything else life requires. Our basic "insurance" should be our right to life! Still we should be able to access additional insurance to insure that the quality of our survivors' lives doesn't change upon our death. The wealthy leave inheritances, the middle class needs insurance, but everyone else will have the "insurance" of an individual right to life. Even a child, orphaned at birth, should have the economic access to sustain itself; though it will need care and nurturing from the community until it reaches maturity.

Chapter 11

OUR ABILITY TO SURVIVE

Perpetual human survival is the ultimate challenge we face as the human race! The measure of any successful society is its' ability to survive any threat to its' existence. Can we survive our own economic extinction? In our case that means we must be prepared to face any economic challenge that could bring about an end to our civilization, or our world, as we know it now. As I gaze into the heavens at night, not even looking for a contact of the third kind, I find it difficult to believe that we are the only intelligent beings in the vastness of the universe. The survival challenges we face have been faced by others before. One day we may find it necessary to leave the confines of this planet in order to perpetuate our species. Are we going to be worthy, or capable, of meeting that challenge?

No matter what you believe; can you honestly look up at the stars at night and believe that we are the only intelligent species capable of reaching beyond their worlds. If we are the only species with the technological expertise to travel between the stars, it is a shame. My hope is that there are others who may have medical or ecological answers that could benefit mankind. It would be in our best interest to develop in a way that we can attract other species by demonstrating our ability to live in peace and work together. Now we would repel any aliens with our anti-social behavior toward each other. Would you like to be the alien responsible for giving the human race the secrets to space travel? They would be unleashing a warring, paranoid, distrusting people with little tolerance for simple differences in skin color, culture, or religion, upon the entire universe.

But even without the aliens we must still find ways to face the forces that man, weather, and pollution have, and can, unleash upon our world. We've overcome environmental challenges that almost destroyed the ozone layer that protects us. Eventually environment won out over greed and expediency and we took the steps that were necessary to reverse the damage. We have the capacity to purify or poison the waters that support life, but economic greed is winning out over the science. We have the power to conserves or pollute the land that brings forth our food and supports our wildlife, and we have chosen to pollute it for economic expediency.

We are capable of producing positive effects on our economic environment if we can remove the cost barriers that prevent the use of new technologies and alternative energy sources. If companies could make use of technology, instead of paying taxes, we can clean our water, land, and air! If we are unsuccessful at taming our environment, it is not as if the world will suffer. We make it bad enough it will kill us and the world will heal itself given the time. It is we who must get along with the world. We can only destroy our own ability to survive! To correct some problems, and minimize others, only our economy stands in our way.

There may be things that could happen to us that we can never control. Celestial events that may one day threaten our civilization, and test our abilities, wait for us in space. Our ultimate goal is to survive when pushed to the brink of extinction. From global warming to unknown threats mankind will eventually face global survival issues that will require a strong global civilization with strong economies in order to overcome inescapable global devastation. We must build an economy that will allow mankind to persevere. Whether or not we survive will depend on our ability to come together and focus our minds and resources on the problem at hand.

Grow up people! Did the fabled Tower of Babble confused more than our tongues? It seems to have confused our minds as well. Otherwise people could not have such definitively diverse and opposing ideas about so many social issues. On many of these matters we must simply agree to disagree but to survive we must find a way to focus our minds, abilities, and resources so that we can address; the ultimate survival issues we may face. We must be able to meet any challenge so that all of our races, cultures, religions, and, most importantly right now, our economies may survive. If we can move beyond the simple task of living every day, we can start planning to survive any future. By providing economic assess to everyone in America, we can remove healthcare barriers, promote education, begin housing distribution, end unemployment, business bailouts, and sustenance cost barriers so we can feed and shelter a global nation. Then we will end poverty, most economically motivated crime, and start working on some of our more deep-rooted and ineradicable social problems.

Accounting for our earnings and our usage are only book keeping task. If you don't earn access to something of value you will not be able to access those items. The value of our productivity shall give us an equal value of access. Good accountability protects our value system and no one is better than we are at counting! How you get to be the head of General Motors – or in any other executive productive position – will still depend upon your personal drive and ambition and, unfortunately – cronyism, nepotism, and racial identification. The truly racist barriers that still exist today will remain as long as men feel superior to each other. Changing people is a battle we hope to win by changing the system that supports us!

The world needs access to the basic necessities of living – shelter, sustenance, education, healthcare, and energy. Even water, phones, electricity, and cablevision, in America, should be here for us to use and not the other way around. Some things we need to have access to all the time and should not be denied because of an inability to pay! Extracting my earning from the pockets of someone else is really a real primitive form of economics. Anything that fails to evolve becomes extinct, including the human race. Let's make a change! Don't let it be the human race that loses the race for survival!

Chapter 12

FIGHTING EVERY WAR WE'RE FIGHTING

Our leaders are good at declaring war on our problems; but winning them has proven to be not so easy. First, let's talk about why we fight! We fight for control! We fight to control the actions, beliefs, property, prosperity, and resources of others. Now let's take a quick look at some of our fights and see how we're doing. On the home front we have the longest ongoing war in the history of mankind. It is a war that has been fought since the dawn of civilization, and that is the war against poverty. Trillions of dollars have been thrown into the war against poverty. Since the beginning of land ownership, which prevented people from living off the land, poverty has been a constant thorn in our sides.

In modern times low cost housing and other social welfare programs have attempted to bridge the poverty gap between the poor and the middle class. Despite our best efforts the number of poor and homeless people continues to grow. We're losing this war, and will continue to lose it, as long as we continue to fight it with tax dollars and charity. As social needs grow, the war on poverty is a war that we cannot afford to stop fighting. The consequences of losing our war on poverty will bring about our end just as it has every civilization that failed to meet the needs of their masses! Abject poverty will bring about REVOLUTION, which is essentially the poor taking over and installing a new aristocracy! Societal wars, like those in the Middle East and elsewhere, are waged between the armies of the rich and the hoards of poor people fighting to not starve! Our society is also vulnerable to social chaos unless we find a way to encompass the economic needs of three hundred million Americans and seven and a half billion people around the world; and counting! Meet the survival needs of the poor and there will never be another social uprising.

We also have our longtime war against crime. We've built and filled about 2000 prisons and continue to build more. But crime continues to spread throughout our society. The yearly cost alone of warehousing two million plus people, at about $40,000 per inmate, is enough to make you realize that we need to address the causes of crime rather than just punish the people who commit them. Yea, we need to wage a war against the *causes* of crime. Deplorable business crimes of low wages to employees, criminal and ineffectual government leadership, greed inspired credit schemes, illiteracy, hunger, and homelessness are good places to start. Maybe then we can stop failing people, and then people will stop failing us! Only our success in addressing the needs of people is going to enable us to defeat crime.

Now, let's move on to the war against drugs! (This should have been included in the war on crime but we gave it its' own paragraph because it has been named as a war by our government!) This war has been desperately waged for many long years. Are we close to winning this war? Let's see? Our prisons are overflowing because we have handed out draconian drug sentences and closed every path to social reintegration of the offenders. We still have drugs on every street in America. By telling our children to just say no to drugs we have acknowledged that we cannot stop them from being sold. Even with a police state and draconian sentencing we are just giving lip service to the problem instead of admitting our total defeat. The fact that drugs are available, everywhere in America, suggest that this war may indeed be lost.

Americans consume tons of marijuana (a natural herb we just call a drug by the way) and millions of other legal and illegal drugs everyday! That much illegal product requires a well organized distribution network. A long time ago there was prohibition of alcohol in this country. People still wanted to drink so illegal activities to supply alcohol grew to historic and tragic proportions. But without drugs, government control over the population would be extremely difficult. Whoever is bringing the drugs into this county is benefiting more than just dollars. They are also keeping racial unrest down and keeping our youth from revolting. They are stripping Americans of much needed economic resources and diverting whole family incomes. Only one entity gains from a population too high to take issue with the state of the economy and the infringement of our civil liberties;

and that entity is the government. Tons of pot everyday are sold across America everyday; never in short supply... you figure it out!

Another war, fought throughout modern history, is the war against homelessness! I think we are losing that war too. Or maybe we are just losing interest in it! Homelessness, tragically, only seems to be a big social concern during the winter. More specifically during the Christmas season when the thought of people facing the elements tugs at our souls and prevents our total seasonal happiness. We can't be happy because deep down inside we know that we won't share our homes with them, no matter how cold they get. I can hardly remember hearing about the homeless any other time of the year; and I'm sure there are homeless people year around.

The war on education has been stalemated by the cost of education and the growing disinterest of a number of our children. The attacks on teachers unions, teachers tenure, and trying to pass the blame for the disillusioned pressured children we send to school, who are not learning, onto the teachers we hire to teach them is simply not fair. It was parents who rejected the reality that corporal punishment is a necessary option to control kids in school. Banning corporal punishment was a mistake of biblical proportions! Peer pressure and bullying have taken a heavy toll on our children. The economic stressors their parents face affect them. The lack of sports programs and extracurricular activities are hurting our children and society is paying the price. How can a child study and focus if they are worried about having dinner or a roof over their heads when they get home. Our older children suffer from a depressing hopelessness about their futures. Seeing the hopelessness of their parents, they face the realization that when school is over they will be competing against their parents for jobs paying meager wages. With dropout rates increasing, educating our children is a war we are losing. There shouldn't be a war to educate our children; it is simply our social obligation.

The war on healthcare was lost without ever being fought. Newer and deadlier diseases are poised to wreak havoc upon the world's populations. With only a third of the world's people having access to processed medications, and modern medical care, needed to fight the spread of disease, we need to solve our economic issues so we can defend our population against disease. In a medical need based economy we can address the needs of the sick and reward the doctors, nurses, and medical technicians that treat us. Now, millions die needlessly and we can only stand by and count the dead.

Now, that leaves the newest war of all; the world war that we're waging against terrorism. Although this war has proven costly in terms of lives and money, it has produced few positive results. We removed , or helped remove, some corrupt, oppressive and egomaniacal dictators, but at what cost; and replaced them with what? For the lives and money we have thrown into this war the threat of terrorism still exists, and the cost of fighting it will continue to rise as the world fall into economic ruin. Another problem with this war is there is no terrorism army to fight. Terrorism is violence or the threat of violence carried out for political purposes. I never could see the purpose killing and maiming because of one's beliefs! All that achieves is making people want to kill you... not listen to what you have to say! We're going to always be terrified of each other if we do not learn to be tolerant of each other. Commonality is how we grow closer. Living common experiences and lifestyles is the best way to bond nations. Making sure our enemies have TVs', microwaves, cell phones, and other things in common with us, should lessen hostilities. We will never be successful fighting terrorism with conventional warfare. The casualties of this war will continue to grow unless we look for peaceful economic solutions. People who work and live well are less likely to fight. Not only do we have human casualties to mourn from this war, we have growing economic casualties as well. The direct effect that the war on terrorism has had on America, our airlines, hotels, oil and other industries, has touched us all and will likely record terrorism in history as causing the most devastating economic holocaust of all time.

Our military involvement in global affairs may sometimes be necessary, and our fighting men and women are brave and superior to most enemy forces. But as economies around the world worsen, how much American blood are we willing to shed in order to right the wrongs and end the political strife in economically failing countries abroad. Our armed forces, though superior, have tired of the constant and seemingly endless bloodshed. As American boys and girls die and are maimed, the American people must demand that lasting peace come from our military interventions around the world.

We should end our continuing occupation of foreign lands. Before the days of almost instant travel, it was necessary to maintain combat ready forces abroad to defend our allies, and interest. Now we can put a hundred thousand troops in the field in a matter of days. Let us bring true peace and order to the world. Let us bring economic reforms that will end the political strife, hunger, murder, disease, and the constant warring of man against man. Millions die every year from war, anger, hate, and rage that devalues the most precious thing we have; human life! WE all hold life dear, but don't cherish it unless it is our own. Life, that most precious gift God has given to us, must be valued by leaders of governments. The lives for which God gave us his only son, so that we would find life everlasting.

These almost perpetual wars have divided this nation, as have the many other wars before it. We face the same question after every fight! How do we end the war and keep America strong? Throwing billions of dollars into Iraq only served to create a new aristocracy and greater animosity among the needy. Our only positive way out of war is to set an example the vanquished are willing to follow. I would like to ask the warring factions to allow us to send workers into their countries to start building roads, water and waste treatment infrastructure, hospitals, schools and food and clothing distribution centers. Pull needy people off the street and put them to work rebuilding their cities and improving *their* human condition! Assure them that all people will share in the economic resources that are available, and that other sources of economic participation will also be made available to them.

Instead of pallets of money we should send homebuilding supplies along with people to help them build. We should have built them an infrastructure using solar power and wind technology. We should have built them water irrigation systems, desalination plants and modern farming tools so they can feed their people. We should have sent them products that would have increased demand for products here at home. We should have sent American made televisions, satellites receivers, washing machines, driers, stoves, clothing, and other commodities that we make in order to make better users of the people in need. American companies could have benefited from the increased demand for products. Just sending pallets of cash is, and was, a bad idea.

People rebuilding a country don't need money if they can get the things that money can buy; and that is product! Think of the boon to the American economy if we had used this terrible war to increase our productivity rather than our tax burdens. We could have added jobs, expanded our tax base, and repaired a few of our own bridges, roads, and public holdings.

We should use foreign aid money to pull men and women off the streets to make them factory, road, and construction workers instead of soldiers and policeman. The brain pool in war torn countries will take years to refill as the best qualified minds and workers have fled the police states we leave behind. People need more then the freedoms of democracy and religion in order to keep the peace and survive. All of our *denied* freedoms have made an additional three and a half million Americans homeless in the greatest country in the world! The workers in Iraq needed jobs and opportunities to keep them too busy to kill, maim, and fester over the frustrations they face. Once they had some economic relief they would need economic stability to ensure the economic existence of every Iraqi. Access to critical infrastructure would alleviate the fear and uncertainty Iraqis have of living and surviving in Iraq after we've gone.

While trying to answer all of the global appeals for American help, we are failing to meet the needs of our own population. By giving so much to others, by giving the lives of our military men and women, and by giving endless monetary support to Iraq and other countries, we only further weaken our own nation! Our society is weak because we turn to charity, too often, to meet the needs of people! Imagine our society as a solid wall standing strong against all forces of man and nature; and let that wall represent the strength that our nation should have. Now, imagine a wall reinforced by many sticks. Sticks representing every charity, every social organization, and every government program that helps us to maintain our society and you can see that we have a very weak social wall. A crumbling wall where people are the stones falling from the cracks in it.

And what of the war we're waging against Mother Nature? We shouldn't be fighting her at all, but we are! We have the technology to greatly curtail our use of fossil fuels, but economic concerns prevent us from pursuing them. We are the aggressor in the war with nature. In this war I hope we are defeated. For if Mother Nature fights back she will shake us off like a mild summer cold. It is we who are at her mercy.

All these wars share one thing in common; they are all a drain on our depleted social economic resources. We have spent trillions of tax dollars and can't claim one total victory out of all these wars! It is time for us to rethink our approach to solving our problems. Throwing bullets and money at them does not work. Maybe we may need to start a few more wars! Maybe we need a war against the **high interest rates** imposed on the poor people of this country. This would help stimulate the economy as shoppers could expect to buy more with their money. If we end the economic transgression perpetrated against the poor, it will strengthen the poor and eventually allow them to recover and gain a foot hold. As long as we have furniture rental places that sell/lease a $200 stove to the desperate buyer for payments totaling $800 dollars or more, and check cashing places that charge from 10 to 25 percent for each check they cash, the poor will continue to be nothing more than a source to plunder and make high profits from. Banks that charge non-customers to cash checks written by their accountholders are taking advantage of the spirit of fair play. High interest rates (money making money) fees and fines are not what building the American (banking) dream was founded upon. We can easily pass legislation to win the war against high interest rates and unfair banking practices. It is a worthwhile and winnable war. Now how many wars is that. Counting our military involvements around the globe and our group and individual crusades for causes, the number is quite considerable. The basic objective of most winners of wars is to divide and conquer the enemy. Our economy is stretched to the breaking point and it had divided us into rich and poor, and will conquer us all.

Maybe we should have a war against bloated egotistical individual personal incomes. How much money is enough for a days' work? Personal drive and ambition is, and should be rewarded. At what point is a fair monetary goal reached? At some point, however, the number's games must stop. Just like in the game of monopoly extreme incomes are capable of bankrupting every other player. We could easily legislate a ceiling on personal wealth without stemming the personal drive and ambition that leads to personal achievement and lifestyles of opulence. We could say that once you accumulated, oh say, TWO BILLION DOLLARS or so, maybe it should then be time for you to retire and give someone else a bite at *that* productive little apple!

Money controls too many of us. Accumulation of "things" is the only thing that stimulates and drives some of us. Cash is just supposed to be a means to an end. It is what the cash can buy for us, or enables us to control, that we really want. Accumulated productivity can easily be translated into the lifestyles we are able to access; but more importantly, to some of us, is the power that having money gives us over other people. The power to open and close economic doors for people, or to enrich them, or control them, is an awesome power. It has proven itself to be more powerful then family relationships marriage bonds or friendships. It has proven to be a weakness in the economic stability of the human race!

That brings us to the second way I propose to solve our economic problems. It is commercial plan that would fit into our current economy and bring about many of the same positive economic changes that our proposed economic rights amendment would. It offers security and stability to people besieged by the economic iniquity of the system we employ. It is a simple plan where people join together to increase their purchasing power and establish a lifeline to protect people from traditional banking fees and fines! It is a cashless, distribution based, economic group where all of the members combine the earnings from their productivity to establish lifestyles and a network safety net. It is a way to provide economic safeguards for every member's lifestyles, under an evolved banking and insurance institution. The simple outline of a profit generating organization I call: **LIFESTYLES FAMILY FINANCIAL MANAGEMENT SERVICES.** This planned economic system also includes built in checks, balances, and safeguards against greed and manipulation; no matter how strong that greed is.

Chapter 13

GIVE ME YOUR TIRED YOUR POOR

America! Home of the brave and land of the free! If you come here illegally you may be brave, but you'll never be really free. The problem with illegal immigration is not the illegal immigrants. The problem stems from the economic problems these workers face in their countries! Countries around the world are all facing much more server the same problems that we are. Their economies are more likely to be struggling from years of relying on acquisition based systems. The older the civilization is the worse off they tend to be economically. The way to fix our immigration problem is to fix the economic problems of the countries these people are fleeing.

Illegal's flee to America to fight off the starvation and hopelessness they face in their countries. Many of them undertake a dangerous journey in order to get here and take advantage of the better chances of success offered in America. Most of the countries these people are fleeing, never made the technological and social leaps that catapulted America into the economic giant we became! If there were satiable economic opportunities in their countries there would be less survival flight to America. Illegal immigrants should be granted refugee status for fleeing to America for their survival. The only way to stem the tide is to extend a new American economic agenda to their countries so that there is no need for them to flee.

And how do we fix the economic problems of the world that have forced millions of economic refugees to flee their homes and families for a chance at survival in America or another country? We need to help them remove the economic barriers that have crippled and stagnated both their, and our, economies. We need to help them start building the healthcare, energy, education, housing, manufacturing, agricultural, and retail infrastructures, at home, that are necessary to provide outlets for their productivity and economic access for their people.

All most people want to do is live, work, and pray that they have economic access to the fruits of their labor. While outsourcing has stripped Americans of millions of needed jobs, the relocated companies did not create sustainable economic access for the workers who are now doing those jobs. Outsourced jobs produce products that must be exported back to America and sold to a shrinking group of American consumers. NAFTA and CAFTA should have focused on seeding, and establishing, new markets instead of greedily outsourcing American jobs so they can pay pennies instead of dollars!

Clothing workers abroad should be able to afford the clothing that they make. Other goods being manufactured abroad could have also been used to elevate the standard of living of workers abroad! If outsourcing had been turned into market expansion, instead of the abject exploitation of workers abroad, American companies could be making American quality products in other countries for *consumption* in those countries. All exported American jobs should have been used to expand and create the once enviable American standards of living around the world. American factories should have seeded Mexico, Europe, Africa, China, and Asia with factories that pay near American wages in order to elevate those countries' economies. American products could then be made for the consumption of the foreign workers who made them. The profits for companies would then have increased by the *volume of sales* rather than by exploiting workers abroad while cutting the throats of the American workers who built the companies in the first place. Paying American workers was good enough to establish the American companies who have now abandoned us and left us with staggering unemployment! By elevating the living standards of foreign workers, in their countries, and paying those workers fairly, foreign workers would probably stay at home. Instead the abject poverty at home continues to force them to flee to America. If we continue to export American jobs so we can pay cents instead of dollars, to foreign workers, foreign workers will continue to flee to America for a real economic opportunity that offers a chance of obtaining the fruits of life that poverty denies!

Until the people motive replaces the profit motive, in business, there will be nothing to prevent the eventual collapse of our economy. America can only support a finite numbers of workers, and those workers need jobs that allow them access to the American Dream. An economic dream, based on the lifestyles we have dreamed of and built, in America. All people dream the same dream. Life, liberty, and the pursuit of happiness are not just American dreams. They are sought after by billions of people around the world!

Illegal immigration is illegal! In the meantime (rather than rounding up and deporting millions of people) the only way for Americans to keep from engaging in un-American conduct is for our government to declare that all existing illegal aliens be granted refugee status because they were forced to flee from poverty. Then, once again, those immortal words etched on our Statue of Liberty will ring true; "Give me your tired you're poor, your huddled massed yearning to breathe free, the wretched refuge from your teeming shore. Send these, the homeless, tempest-tossed to me. I lift my lamp beside the golden door." Let America reach out with a new economic paradigm that will lift billions from poverty!

Our government has an obligation to fulfill. They must protect the shores of America. The American people deserve protection from all forms of invasion. The negative impact of the wage battle being fought on American soil is hurting Americans. What we have worked so hard to build is being usurped by the companies that take advantage of illegal workers willing to earn far less than Americans in order to stay in America. Our government should be standing firm against this economic onslaught that can only further weaken our economy. They should punish the greedy businesses that are reaping profits from the battle. Only then can all Americans survive, economically, in America!

Chapter 14

GREATER THAN US

First, let me dissuade any fears that anyone may have about my organization, P.O.W.E.R.S., or I, being in any way against religion. I'm talking about how we let our religions get in our way! The problems we are having "connecting" with people of other religions are caused by us not being tolerant and understanding. It is generally known and accepted that more death and destruction has been visited upon the world in the name of God, then for any other reason.

Religions are supposed to promoted love, peace, and our understanding of something greater then ourselves. If I don't fully get someone's religion I simply relate to those people on a basic human level. The human ability each of us has to understand the difference between good social behavior and bad should be enough to keep us from killing each other; but it doesn't. Religion is often the reason we abandon the basic human instinct to identify with, and have compassion for, each other. As long as mankind has existed we should have conquered our inability to live among each other! Religious hatred should be nonexistent among modern thinking men! From nations hating nations, to neighbor hating neighbor we are failing religion 101. From religion hating religion, to church hating church, religious differences have caused hatred and death. Let's build a better world that allows each person in it to live and worship as they will while we all enjoy life... God's greatest gift!

Our leaders have been reduced to using religion against us to stir support for their elections, their political agendas, and their wars. Religious zealots have used their religions to justify the murder and maiming of innocent men, women, and children around the world. It is time for people across America, and around the world, to seek peace, understanding, and have respect for the value of life *because* of our religious beliefs.

I know Americans who are full of hatred for all Arab nations. They think our government should "turn the desert into a glass plate!", with our nuclear superiority. Some of our religious leaders are so fearful that they can't think about finding peace with people who only worship differently! We will never grow as a global society if we continue to have too great an emphasis on religion! Kill a father and you turn his child against you, and the killing will never stop! In Belfast it took the love of mothers to stop the killing! Thousands of young people had been killed and it was mothers that said enough was enough! All killing is unnecessary if we can only accept our differences! There is no religious dogma, no ideology, worth killing for! We teach our children to have tolerance and understanding of each other because we understand that they are like insects; without natural compassion, when they are young. Without compassion or understanding very young children can easily hurt each other. We adults, on the other hand, don't have the excuse of youth; we are just mean, intolerant, and immature! Part of maturing is figuring out ways to have differences of opinion without resorting to violence. Might and numbers of followers doesn't make you right either! No matter what your religious belief why can't you just respect life enough to preserve it at all cost? If you are alive today you know what your life means to you; how precious it is, and how fragile it is. How can you disregard the value of a life that is not yours? If you take a life in the name of God then you do not cherish Gods greatest gift!

Don't look for an economic bail out from God either. He wants us to worship him not come to him begging him to solve problems we created! When we were cast from the Garden of Eden he did not give us money to purchase the things he gave us. If he had created an economic system I'm sure it would have been distribution based rather than acquisition based! Genesis 3:22: And the LORD God said, Behold, the man is become as one of us, to know good and evil: and now, lest he put forth his hand, and take also of the tree of life, and eat, and live forever. With that, God summed up what he expected from us. The tree of life; which I believe is knowledge, put us in charge of our existence. Our punishment was to leave Eden and go do for ourselves what God had intended to do for us. And by the statement above we also know that we have no excuses for doing wrong to each other. We know good and evil! Everything else we have had to learn!

We cannot be so indifferent to the plight other people? We must rise above our animal instincts to prey upon each other. How can you take another's life, when you know what your death would mean to the people who love you? If you see on the news a report of someone's untimely death shouldn't you feel some sadness because a fellow human is dead? The thought of causing someone's death should never enter our minds! Poverty, hunger, and disease aren't going to be cured by God; it's up to us. Religions grisly history of death is because men acting as religious leaders have used their office to breed hatred and intolerance throughout the world! More people have been killed in the name of God than in all the other wars, and natural catastrophes combined. Religious wars, like other anti-social crimes, will probably, regrettably, go on until the end of the time of man. But maybe if we can end the economic battles people face, maybe then we may be able to concentrate on other anti-morality issues.

In a P.O.W.E.R.S. based economy "practicing religion" will still be possible for believers, who will face fewer economic barriers to prevent them from fellowshipping and worshiping. Any group, founded as a religion, will still get economic access from the support of their members, as they do now. The congregation of the church will grant the church staff their economic access. Churches will be the only non-profit organizations to survive this economic evolution revolution, and will operate as they do now.

Other economic support based religious charities will, and should gladly, go the way of the dinosaurs, as they will no longer be needed in a working and structured economic system. All charities should be trying to work themselves out of a job anyway! Success, to charities, is to no longer be needed. But until the dedicated workers, who have helped shore up the crumbling economic wall of society, can find jobs in the private sector we will continue to grant their economic access to them.

I looked up into the heavens one night and saw a star as bright as the Star of David that guided the three wise men to Bethlehem. If Jesus has come back and is in his infancy what do we want him to find when he grows up? Will he be able to walk among us and feel safe and secure? Will he find us worthy to be called: Children of God? Can we do for ourselves what God was going to do for us? I think that we can! The ability is within us.

It seems that much of our population has also given in to projections in Revelations rather than preparing for revolutions as they accept that these days may indeed be the end of days.

I can't believe that God, or the universe for you non believers, would create people capable of all we have accomplished, and endowed us with free will, just to see us give in to some preordained fatalistic end. If you must believe in something turn your page to Genesis 3:22,23 where God proclaimed after He gave us clothes to clothe us, "Behold, for the man has become as one of us." Believe in the success we've had with our medical and technological achievements! Believe that as God's children there is no task too great for us to achieve. Only our belief in our own ability to overcome the shortcomings of our economy is wanting. Life 101 should be an easy A for the children of God!

Chapter 15

KILLING THE CREDIT MONSTER

I try to do little complaining, about our economy, during the writing of this book but on the subject of credit it will be hard for me not to complain! Credit has become such a significant problem in our global economy that it deserves its' own chapter in this book. Once a simple mechanism that allowed consumers to stretch out payments for major purchases, credit has morphed into an unfair, uncontrolled entity that can affect a persons' employment, their ability to rent housing, our governments' ability to operate, and our society's ability to grow! Our government allows businesses to wield credit like a double edged sword, gouging risky customers with credit problems and raising interest rates as high as 99%; for people desperate enough to sign on the dotted line! Bad credit doesn't prevent you from getting credit! It just makes you a target for the greedy lenders that prey on the poor.

If credit is the economic "devil", we are facing, the greatest trick it ever played on mankind is called "Amortized Principal and Interest payments: Amortized, for us consumers, means, "To reduce a debt by installments". In the beginning P & I payments were an equal number of principle and interest payments that collected and equal dollar amount of principle and interest, over the term of the loan. It then morphed into the current monstrous system which keeps us perpetually underwater in our loans. When our government allowed interest to be collected in greater amounts then the principle paid on a loan, credit became the bane of our credit ruled existence! Interest payments should NEVER have been allowed to exceed the amount of principle paid at any time; hence the original term Principle *and* Interest is no longer true!

I added this chapter to the book last because credit is the true terrorist that American workers fear. When the underpaid walk into a store, where they will need to use credit, they're afraid of their paycheck being exploited by high down payments and high interest rates they will be subjected to. They're afraid of credit denial, but equally afraid of being accepted. Credit is the most recent tool of our economy to be turned against us. It is an effective way for the rich to gain astronomical personal wealth while keeping the people they underpay poor! We are so deep in debt that our total credit is greater than the actual amount of physical currency in circulation. While our government turns a blind eye to growing interest rates, credit that denies people employment or access to higher education, credit is wreaking havoc with our social bottom line... the lives of people.

Our government is the largest debtor in America, with the worst track record for payment, but it continues to get favorable interest rates from banks and other lenders while our national debt grows exponentially! Banks and lenders lean on the underpaid to fill their coffers and our government sits idly by without the will or the ideas necessary to stop the economic oppression of billions of people! P.O.W.E.R.S. people are mostly the poor who, until now, were without voice and without any choice but to bear the burdens of survival!

No old time haggling or negotiations are allowed in this stringent, cold, economy! Many "credit risk" have signed outrageous credit contracts knowing that repayment would be almost impossible for them. "Maybe I can pay it off long as no one gets sick, the car doesn't break down, and I don't lose my job or become a victim of crime." We are creating a nation of creditors and debtors and losing sight of the dream everyone is supposed to be working for... the American dream! Credit has become an autonomous, uncontrollable monster that is devouring and devaluing people whom it should be, simply, helping to extend payments on a purchase!

When people with millions of dollars can go broke and end up in debt, then the American dream is too fragile anyway! Physical currency is our enemy, and it uses the greed it inspires to cut the social ties that bind us, and isolates us in our individual credit quagmires. As long as we continue to extract our livings from each other's pockets we will be forced to play the numbers game while we continue to kick our dead horse of an economy. By maintaining the status quo we will never reach a level of economic existence worthy of, or capable of, encompassing the children of God. The need for credit, like physical currency, has become a barrier between our productivity and our usage of what we produce. Large social entities like our governments, schools, and healthcare systems, will never realize their fullest potential as long as they depend upon credit, fees, fines, and taxes, from the rest of us, in order to exist. Our social welfare system, courts, police departments, and prison systems are already inundated with the results of our economic failures and their cost is growing along with our needs for justice and social economic parity. We spend valuable economic resources trying to control things like the illegal distribution of plants that anyone can grow, while the crime of credit continues unabated! We've wasted more billions on pork barrel legislation that fattens the pockets of the constituents politicians enrich for the dollars they're going to need to remain in office. And we destroy families by requiring struggling families to be without adult males before they can qualify for public assistance, even if it means that those families will need even more financial assistance.

Uncontrolled interest rates and growing credit should be policed as they are poised to make our courts and prisons explode as businesses continue to economically oppress people trying to access and maintain the barest standard of living possible. While individuals profit millions our government does nothing to stop the disparity between employers and workers. For the eighty-nine percent of people convicted of purely economic crimes, society failed them long before they failed society. So careful whom you call a criminal now days; they could be your father, mother, sister, or brother and remember that when you see crimes on the increase remember that it is the human need to survive that precipitates it. The will to live indoors, eat food, and be clothed is primeval and stronger than any law! Even the threat of prison is favorable over the possibility of starvation, homelessness, and economic deprivation! In order for one of us to survive, it must be possible for all of us to survive.

The philosophy behind this. economic solution will erase all individual and government debt by simply giving all creditors access based on their accounts receivables. They will be paid for their productivity. Home renters will be given the value due for their properties and those properties will then be repaired, or replaced, and used to end homelessness! To be successful civilization builders the only bottom line we can consider is the human one. What is good for mankind must be the driving force behind our economy, our governments, and the decisions that we make. We must replace greed with compassion, economic fears with optimism, physical currency and credit with structured economic access based upon group and individual needs and productivity. We are either going to be good producers and users, or face the possibility of mass starvation and homelessness. The decision is ours to make!

Chapter 16

RUNNING OUT OF TIME

Time *IS* ticking away for humanity! There are fatalists among us who believe that the end of our existence is near and that nothing we do will make any difference. I guarantee you that we will become extinct if we do nothing! But what if our end doesn't come for a very long time? Are we to stop meeting life's challenges and stop evolving just because our generation may be the last? Shouldn't we prepare just in case we survive?

The big picture, as I see it, is for us to *quickly* overcome our intrinsic social and economic problems so that we can meet the challenges that nature, or the universe, can throw at us. We have to plan, and act, to meet every threat to the existence of humanity. To survive an ice age or other catastrophic climatic changes, we should be building shelters around the globe to protect and increase the yields from our vulnerable agricultural systems. We should put millions of acres of land under secure, multi tiered, and climate controlled enclosures so that our supply of food will not be dependent upon the graces of good weather. We should start protecting our critical electrical infrastructure from inclement weather by making the technology stronger or by putting it securely and safely underground with our plumbing and telephone lines. And wouldn't it be nice to have highways and runways that were electrically heated so that we could safely use them in inclement weather. We have so many bigger fish to fry and so much that we need to improve upon, and implement if only we could get over the cost barriers, corporate and individual greed, poverty, war, and crime that have plagued us since the beginning of time.

Economic evolution, no matter how unlikely it sounds, is the only way we can eradicate our intrinsic economic problems and perpetuate the human race. I get few responses to my correspondences because people LOVE money! It is tangible and exciting when held in abundance. It is soothing to know you have enough of it to have security for yourself and your family, and it is the substance of our fantasies and the cure we work for and hope will fall into our lives. People, MONEY, the physical kind, is the bane of our existence. It is holding us back in every way. We must free humanity of physical currency and let value, and our ability to account for our usage of what we produce, be the currency of the future. There are many ways to access legitimate markets and we must find that rewarding and fulfilling enough. We cannot live for money! It is literally destroying us. We must live for each other. The people motive must replace the profit motive as our reason for living.

Yes time is ticking away and we must act now or be driven into extinction by our failure to evolve economically! Wanting to live and enjoy your wealth won't be possible if we fail economically! We will all live or perish together!. We must start to plan if we are going to survive. Thousands of years of monies failure to provide should be enough for all of us. If we are going to go on we must start a dialogue about an economic paradigm for change and not be content to prattle on about budgets, taxes, and loopholes until our time runs out.

We are children of a God who created the wonders of life and all the world and universe we have to behold. Let us endeavor to create a civilization and economic system worthy of the children of God.

Chapter 17

THE FIX

Those preaching austerity and smaller government are clearly visionless if they can't see that they cannot put decades of progress back into a box. I believe that all our representatives, and Presidential candidates, should run as independents; running solely on the merits of their political agendas and beliefs. Our two party system has been rendered ineffectual because of special interest influence and partisan politics. With every politician raising and spending millions of dollars to wage a political campaign for jobs paying less than two hundred thousand dollars, how can the process be fair and honest. If I were to wage a political campaign it would be waged as cheaply as possible. I would not burden my fellow Americans for money; only for their votes. I would do this because I would want to be elected for my ideas. It is time we return government to the wise; not the wealthy!

What is the purpose in trying to undo decades of progress and human growth? Simple, they see that their policies have forced millions onto the welfare rolls and even working class families have become more and more dependent on our already overtaxed charities and social programs. These singularly satisfied wealthy people just don't want to give charity to the growing numbers of poor they have created! The number of people willing and able to give to charity is not keeping pace with the growing number of people in need of social charity.

Those running with promises of maintaining a public safety net are equally visionless trying to undo the future of human growth. Both groups have failed to look outside the box they were born into and neither has tried to develop ideas that can move us forward. Over the last thirty years I first mused, then studied, and then developed the economic paradigm that I am now propagating. My: **Proposed Amendment to the Constitution of**

the United States of America to Establish Rights, is my offering for the quick and long term stabilization of our economic system.

Many Americans are just beginning to realize that other nations are tied to Americas' successes and failures. The threats of the collapse of our global economies like those in Greece, Africa, Spain, and the European Union will also strike death blows to the US economy. Many world leaders are going door to door with their hands out waiting for America to lead. It's time we did.

I would also run for office with a promise on my lips for the American people. A promise to increase our massive government spending maintaining hope and healing the human spirit. I believe that we must repair and expand our survival infrastructure and do whatever is necessary to preserve and enrich human life. I believe in spending whatever is necessary to address human suffering when natural or unnatural catastrophes occur here, or around the world. And I believe that governments taxation of corporations, businesses, and individuals, who all wish to avoid paying the taxes anyway, is unnecessary in a modern economic age.

We are not stuck with the trillions of dollars in debt or the failed economic paradigm that has left us with poverty and staggering unemployment, against a backdrop of prosperity and opulence. I believe that our trillions of dollars of government and individual debt is a simple accounting chore and a situation that can be eliminated along with the taxes we don't want to pay. To reach these goals we must move now to evolve economically. However, until an economic evolution can be legislated into existence, taxes are the bitter pill we must all take to support the workings of our government; while it conducts the business of America. And the business of America is ensuring that Americans are secure in their freedom and secure in their futures.

The party politics, bickering, and pomposity taking place in Washington can only be corrected if Americans elect to have an economic system that promotes self-sufficiency, not social dependency. A system that will cripple economically motivated crime by removing the ambiguous medium of exchange which supports it; in favor of simple accounting practices and the use of plastic access cards. Social security, Medicaid, healthcare, housing, education are all areas where our government has failed to produce a fraction of the stability necessary for us to be successful as social engineers. In a system that does not need social programs there would be no need for taxes or a large social safety net!

We have massive unemployment and business managers who seek to save money by slashing jobs. Everything in our economy is dependent on money and everyone wants to keep it for themselves. Our economy is in a constant state of opposition with itself. To be successful, as the human race, we need an economic system that supports all of us in the same way that nature supports life around us. As long as we maintain the *important* aspects of our free enterprise system, which are our personal drive and ambition, our productivity, and a value based system of distribution, no one should be in opposition to these plans. We will keep our honor, integrity, pride, and craftsmanship and abandon greed, hatred, ignorance, and racism; and we will still have an expectation of being able to obtain a lifestyles of opulence through our individual and collective productivity. Through economic evolution we can make a productivity, value, and distribution based economic system work. While I personally favor the cashless, distribution based economic system, I envision, without the problems we are have providing jobs for millions of workers. Job creation and government spending now force me to intercede in our current economic system's woes.

To create jobs we need a business model with formulas that guarantees job creation. One formula that needs to be injected into this economy is a new compensation paradigm that will satisfy those who need jobs, and those who provide them. In an idealistic distribution based economy no taxes are needed, only granted economic access, but here I try to inject a formula that will create jobs needed to preserve our acquisition based economic system until we are ready to evolve economically to a distribution based system.

1. Any jobs bill introduced into our economic system should solidify that system and limit the need for endless political economic manipulations. It should include structured tax incentives that will inspire businesses to do more hiring. We need a jobs bill that insures that workers receive fair wages for an honest day's work. Tax incentives should also be given based on the amount of benefits and wages paid to their employees.

The more productivity the management of a company is responsible for the lower their corporate tax rate should be. A company like Wal-Mart, because of their sheer number of employees, could easily qualify for the minimum corporate tax rate of 20% if:

a.   **None of their employees require public assistance of any kind.** If your companies management sits at the multi-million or billion dollar round tables, then your employees should be able to live without any public assistance. We have to many people working and on welfare and this is an issue we must address if we are to create jobs.

b.   **The company can lower their tax rate by providing employee-family healthcare with no more than 6% employee contribution.**

c.   **The company can lower their tax rate if they purchase a majority of their supplies and products from American suppliers to increase demand and spur American manufacturing.**

d.   **Companies can also lower their tax rate by lowering their energy footprint by buying close to their markets to reduce transportation and energy cost.**

2.   **Executive compensation** also requires a comprehensive tax formula to prevent abuses by people who write their own paychecks. While I would prefer a ceiling on yearly, and lifetime, compensation in an acquisition based economic system, no one would support that. This is a formula that can limit the economic disparity between employer and employee. Companies will pay higher taxes if their labor force is reduced by cost cutting modernization. In a distribution based system I could care less about the number of zeros in a personal bank account; only that it does not contribute to mass poverty.

a.   If you make your money as a Wall Street investor you will pay the highest corporate tax rate of all because you make money from investing in the labors of others. A higher tax rate is only fair for money made this way does not create jobs. Employees are cost factors that affect an investors bottom line. This will not appeal to the Wall Street crowd who seem to think the accumulation of money is some sort of game. But they are only a small part of us and will have to adjust to benefit the masses. Those who employ few people but make billions of dollars from their *productivity* should be taxed at the highest tax rate possible. These people will pay the maximum corporate taxes and higher personal taxes according to their corporate and personal income.

3. Companies operating outside the US and importing products for sale in American stores will be taxed at a higher tax rate then companies who buy American products to sale.

a. Companies will be taxed higher if the wages they pay foreign worker do not help elevate the standards of living of the workers they employ abroad. Their foreign workers will then, eventually, make products to be consumed by a legion of new consumers in foreign countries. This is the way NAFTA and CAFTA should have worked. Then we could have kept American jobs in America and gained tax cuts by expanding productivity and prosperity abroad.

b. Companies with only a foreign address should lose all tax incentives of being based abroad. These are just tax cheaters.

The social tensions we face over teacher, police, fire, and other public workers' compensation can be easily solved in a distribution based economic system because their services will no longer be labeled non-profit. In an acquisition based system, like we currently employ, their compensation still comes from taxes and those taxes come from the same people who already think they pay too much tax. People will not be opposed to tax formulas that they can adhere to and make legitimate adjustments so that they can legitimately qualify for greater tax breaks.

4. We need OUR government to spend as much as it can to increase product demand and put Americans back to work. We need OUR government to start spending on needed, and necessary, repairs to our physical infrastructure! American government spending must facilitate the expansion of our critical transportation, housing, education, energy, and healthcare infrastructures to insure that they are available when needed.

5. The jobs crisis is exasperated by a debt crisis that is caused, in part, by the way we have manipulated credit. Credit was once only a way to extend payment for high value purchases. Principal and interest payments were not amortized so that most of the interest is collected at the start of a loan. This one change, in what was once a successful economic paradigm, keeps

debtors from accruing equity in their homes and has negatively affected every kind of ownership we have from cars, to furniture, and appliance sales; and has created an enormous home rental, used car, and furniture and appliance rental markets. This breaks a constitutional right that we had to life, liberty, and the pursuit of happiness. Credit must be tamed if an acquisition based economy is to survive.

6. Any jobs bill must also include the decriminalization of marijuana and an overhaul of our drug bloated prison labor industry. It is impossible for Americans to maintain two separate standards of law where there is no federal prosecution for possession of marijuana in some states and prosecution for it in others. Prison labor is undercutting legitimate wage earners and many of those jobs are needed by free Americans.

In a distribution based economic system OUR government would have the inexhaustible economic resources needed to start projects that will heal America and renew the American spirit. Since there would be no taxes those unwilling to help others can fade back into their worlds of blissful ignorance about the plights of others and just enjoy the rewards of their productivity. To emerge from this economic chaos a better nation we must build and explore; not run and hide. We must continue to exemplify the American commitment to excellence, originality, hope, and, most importantly, American leadership, once the envy of the rest of the world.

Our constitutional "inalienable rights to life, liberty, and the pursuit of happiness", as Americans, is being infringed upon by a few loud, singularly satisfied people who are only interested in self instead of community. They fail to realize that we cannot exist without each other. The anguish they chose to inflict on the masses with their devastating cuts to social programs, and job shutdowns may hasten their own demise. The hunger, sickness, and ignorance they want to inflict on our nation, coupled with human dismay and loss of hope, has historically, and is as we speak, leading to global social upheaval, rebellion, and revolution. What makes them think Americans will just continue to take it and do nothing. American police and military men and women will not stand in the way of peaceful social change. They will not protect the money and lives of the rich if Americans decide that freedom must once again be fought for!

The productivity and services that go into making up our GDP must be supplemented by inclusion of the productivity of government workers, police, firemen, and our valued public school teachers. The things we sell are not the only contribution some of us see productivity and value in. All of us need economic access! It is not fair to not include the value of vast social entities that do not generate capital, but which are very important to the wellbeing of our society.

It is easy to see that the shortcomings of this economic system have left us with millions of people who do essential jobs but don't contribute to making up the GDP. The labor of our teachers, firefighters, military personnel, our local, state, and federal government workers must be incorporated into our capitalist system or capitalism will fail. This creates a huge deficit of producers of products to the number of users of products and services produced. Our only answer now is to continue putting a huge tax burden on the labor of production and service workers.

We need to stop extracting our livings from each others' pockets; with a few pockets getting the lions' share of the revenues we generate. We all need to access the products and services we produce. To create our GDP we to add the productivity of our non-producing workers as an accounting exercise and give them a like amount of usage to sustain themselves. We say that teachers, the police, fire workers, military, and government workers are non-profit making workers and in our current paradigm they will require tax dollars to get a paycheck. That's only true because we don't know how to make their contributions count in an acquisition based economy. Our government, teachers, and other public servants provide *indispensable,* productive, contributions to our society and we have to place more than a zero value on their productivity and services. In a distribution based economy the access people are granted will come from their measured productivity and it will not be a tax burden on the rest of us.

We make it work by making everyone's labor provide for them. You access the value of your productivity as established by your labor and the law. Taxes are not the answer so it is time to move on. Let us leave our children a stable economic system and a bright, competitive, rewarding future for their children.

The End

{From the original Constitution}

"WE THE PEOPLE of the United States, in Order to form a more perfect Union, establish Justice, insure domestic Tranquility, provide for the common Defense, promote the general Welfare, and secure the Blessings of Liberty to ourselves and our Posterity, do ordain and establish this Constitution for the United States of America."

My Favorite Quote again

"It is eloquently stated by Ambrose, the magnificent fourth-century bishop of Milan, who thundered:"Think you that you commit no injustice by keeping to yourself alone what would be the means of life to many. It is the bread of the hungry you cling to; it is the clothing of the naked you lock up; the money you bury is the redemption of the poor."

Quote from the original Declaration of Independence

"We hold these truths to be self-evident, that all men are created equal, that they are endowed by their Creator with certain unalienable Rights that among these are Life, Liberty and the pursuit of Happiness. — That to secure these rights, Governments are instituted among Men, deriving their just powers from the consent of the governed, — That whenever any Form of Government becomes **destructive of these ends**, it is the Right of the People to alter or to abolish it, and to institute new Government, laying its foundation on such principles and organizing its powers in such form, as to them shall seem most likely to affect their Safety and Happiness."

PROPOSED AMENDMENT TO THE CONSTITUTION OF THE UNITED STATES OF AMERICA TO ESTABLISH ECONOMIC RIGHTS

Section I

WE THE PEOPLE of the United States of America are still trying to build a more perfect Union, establish Justice, insure domestic Tranquility, provide for the common defense, promote the general Welfare, and secure the Blessings of Liberty to ourselves and our Posterity.

It is our duty to continue trying to establish goals that were made pinned by the blood of our founders during their quest for independence. An independence they intended for us to enjoy. Because they were successful, in gaining our independence, we now have the ability, and the duty, to exercise the rights won. In order to bring about social-economic changes that will end economic dependence, and the greed that perpetuates it, we do hereby submit this Proposed Amendment to the Constitution of the United States of America. This amendment is sorely needed to establish perpetual basic economic rights for every citizen of this country that we can eventually, spread to the world. By establishing our basic economic rights we can free our nation from the economic chaos we are currently immersed in.

Our founding fathers, during their fight for our independence, could not have foreseen the need for the economic rights proposed herein. Perhaps they felt that "freedom" would spawn true social-economic bliss. What must we do to establish a better economic system? We must establish the basic economic rights that are needed in our time, as our forefathers did for the civil rights that were needed in theirs. Their monumental goal of freedom could not have been accomplished without them having, first, realized the need for that freedom. Once they realized their need, they took the necessary steps to secure it forever. Our need for a stable economy is one that we do realize; and one that our current economic manipulations cannot fulfill. Ours must be a new solution that is sound, fair, and obtainable.

We, the People of The United States of America do, hereby, mandate that this legislation be passed for the institution of these extremely significant economic rights. In reaching the goals of this amendment we will bring about an end to the, seemingly, insurmountable economic iniquities that have thrust our once mighty nation into an abyss of constant economic upheaval and manipulation. These proposed economic rights are needed to stabilize our decaying economy and restore hope to the millions of people who are overcome, everyday, by the enormity of the economic iniquities they face. Only by legislating economic rights can we bring about an end to hundreds of years of economic instability and iniquity. By creating a cashless, value based, system of productivity and distribution, we can create a more user-friendly economy. Any new economic strategy will offer a new set of challenges. None of them will be life threatening.

The important thing is that an economic evolution will allow us to build an economic foundation necessary to support the masses. Millions of people depend upon a viable economy in order to survive. Among its many other benefits will be the tax-free, welfare free, and debt free economy that we can create. An accounting economy unlike any we have historically employed.

By establishing immediate economic access, to shelter, food, education, and healthcare, we can then concentrate on phasing out any use of physical currency, without adversely affecting business or peoples' lives. While government tax offices and the banking community prepare for their changing roles, tight restraints should be placed on the use of any physical currency at all. Once restricted the use of physical currency should be limited to specifically authorized and legal transactions. Installation of access machines and conversion of ATM machines should eventually make all physical currency transactions unnecessary.

The struggle for life has taken many Americans to the brink of economic extinction. We want to put into motion a plan to prevent any further loss of life, prosperity, or access to the American Dream; that our current economic system cannot maintain. With so much of the world seeking economic assistance, much of it from us, it is imperative that we take steps to lead the world out of economic purgatory.

Our present economic answers have only served to build more prisons and increase our, already, heavy tax burdens; as many suffering Americans are forced to seek an economic existence by less than honorable means. From cheating on income taxes to welfare fraud and organized crime, our economic deviations proved to have a common catalyst; the quest for physical currency, and what it can buy. It is a quest responsible for ninety-eight percent of all our crime. From the highest corporate and public offices to the lowest labor position, the quest for money has led to every deviation in human behavior. The lures of cash, and the temptations associated with it, have tested us throughout time. Money has turned a mother against a child, a sister against a brother, and a husband against a wife.

If we are to successfully evolve, economically, it will be necessary for us to change our economic focus from one based on a cost factor to one based on a human factor. Once the yoke of economic iniquity is lifted from our society we can freely pursue the happiness, and freedoms, that our forefathers envisioned we would find.

Success in our society is measured by our personal drive and ambition that leads to our economic strength. It is important to us how much economic access we have because it establishes and maintains our lifestyles. The accumulation of dollars and cents is only symbolic of our economic strength; and because of our banking methods it isn't restricted to a physical embodiment. Cash isn't as important to us as it was thirty, twenty, or even ten years ago. Now we are able to shop without physical currency and the eventual phasing out of physical currency is a logical progression of our economic growth. As long as we protect our value system, exemplified by difference in our lifestyles, then our basic economic ideals and our value system will remain intact. Our quest for a life-style of opulence will still be obtainable and maintainable.

Our technology has advanced far beyond the abilities of our economic system. We can make a heart, put it in a body, and expect it to work; but we can't manage to feed and shelter the millions of hungry, and homeless, men, women, and children across the country. By using our advanced technology we can allow everyone to make legitimate purchases, buy homes, cars, or anything else we produce without the use of physical currency. Our cash based economy has failed to fulfill even our minimum social economic requirements. Using cash, we have failed to establish a system that benefits, and sustains our many members and the many needs of our society. The financial machines we use everyday have proved beneficial to us. To get these machines to simply record our productivity, and calculate how much access we have used, is simply a matter of programming.

Along with our technology we must now exercise, our vision and wisdom to secure our perpetual existence; by spelling out the economic rights which will sustain us forever. To establish basic economic rights the Congress of the United States of America will draft and enact laws to establish those rights, which will include:

a. The right to shelter.

When walking down almost any street in America you can find an empty house. Our homeless problem can be solved simply by establishing an equitable housing distribution system; based upon, but not limited to, our productivity; longevity at being productive and our individual housing needs. What we have is a housing distribution problem not a homeless problem.

When we go into a Realtors office, or bank, looking to buy a house the first thing they do is establish how much house we can afford, based upon our income. This, among other factors, establishes the price range of the houses we can shop for. A housing distribution system will use the same criteria to distribute homes as we use to buy them. As our productivity increases so does our desire for more substantial property. "Moving up" is part of the American Dream. The property we vacate can then be redistributed to someone else "moving up" too.

There are many property owners with rental properties intended to provide long-range income for them. This property ranges from single-family dwellings to vast apartment complexes. Even though rents will no longer be collected, property owners will still receive the economic rewards that come from providing their rentals. Many single-family dwellings will eventually become family owned as ownership becomes easier to achieve. Housing rentals will eventually be phased out, and apartments will eventually be sold as condominiums. The builders only want the economic access necessary to maintain and sustain their own life-styles, and the economic access to continue building and providing housing properties. Rental payments will become mortgage payments and owners will still have the long-range income they desired.

b. The right to subsistence.

Food is a necessary right for every citizen. We will all benefit from a society that is well nourished. Our past efforts to deal with the problems of hunger, sincere, as they have been, have not been able to end hunger. Charity has filled many empty stomachs, and is well meaning; but there is nothing as demoralizing as standing in a food line with a slip of paper, or standing in a grocery line with a hand full of food stamps, just to get something to eat. It is a meal without dignity. The fact that more working families in this country need food stamps, to make ends meet, is a sad commentary about the economic advances we've made as a society. Ending hunger is as simple as establishing economic access for everyone.

We live in a society that wastes tons of food every day. Efficient food management could feed millions of people. Some may feel that feeding the world will create food shortages from sheer numbers, but the abundance of food can best be realized at your local grocery store. Just walk down the aisles. Most shelves are full, and seven to ten rows deep. We have a food distribution problem, not a food shortage problem.

c. The right to healthcare.

The healthcare problem is well known to the millions of Americans who have to live without it. From the cradle to the grave every American is in need of healthcare. Healthcare is something that must be accessible to everyone. Doctors, nurses, and the many dedicated specialist and technicians who treat us, deserve to live a lifestyle free of economic worry. Nothing is too good for those who help preserve life.

This amendment charges the Congress of the United States of America to establish structured economic access for everyone, including those in the healthcare industry. Within the healthcare industry economic access is based upon many factors. When a doctor graduates from medical school his or her grades, based upon his or her personal drive and ambition, establishes their professional status and their personal level of productivity. A graduate with good grades can usually expect to get a better position, and earn a better life-style than one with marginal grades. Economic disparity is good for competition.

With everyone in the healthcare industry able to obtain and maintain the lifestyle they earn and have come to expect, then every American can receive the medical care necessary to promote a long and healthy life. We can still carry insurance to protect our families from a change in lifestyle, should something happen to us, but we must, and will, provide quality health care for everyone in the country.

d. The right to education

Education is the heart of human existence. Every human mind must be allowed to reach its fullest potential. That is why we must make the value of our educators contribution, of teaching our children, a tangible contribution to our GDP that allows teachers to establish and maintain lifestyles from the products and services the rest of us provide. Taxing all of us to pay for teachers has proven to be unsustainable in a taxed based system. In a distribution based economic system public employees can feel that their labors have value and that they are contributing to the economy and cannot be labeled a public burden. Teacher unions will give teachers a voice to let legislators know how many schools we need and how many teachers we need to hire. Allowing our educators to educate without worrying about homeless children, hungry children, and children at risk, will benefit all of humanity by keeping our workforce educated, capable, competative, and efficient.

f. The right to energy

Something as important as energy must eventually be removed from the private sector because energy morally belongs to the people of the world. Profit based energy concerns harm the land, pollute it at will, and buy our governments so they can receive subsidies on top of their staggering earnings. The right to use energy will allow every home to be warmed and cooled when necessary. If we use our smart technology we can stretch our energy to meet the needs of seven and a half billion people. We can also move forward with alternative energies that face a cost barrier that has been created to keep fossil fuels profitable.

g. The right to economic access.

Productivity assessment, coupled with usage accountability, will enable us to secure our economic existences while enhancing the lifestyles of every American. No longer will we exist only to pay utility, phone, grocery, mortgage, education, cable, and other bills. Under this new economic system bills will become a matter of simple accounting. The advancements in technology we achieve, and the products we create and produce, will finally be here for us instead of us being here for them.

If our currency-based economy had progressed far enough we would be able to pay off things like utility bills and telephone bills. With billions of dollars in the bank, the month you die you will still get utility and phone bills because we didn't take our cash based economic system far enough. We have failed to reach the basic economic goals proposed in this amendment. We have failed to reach the point where the things we work hard for are protected from being stolen or lost. The fragile nature of our economy forces us to safeguard the money that makes our world go around; and we spend millions just to protect it.

The purpose of the economic changes, proposed herein, is to launch an all out attack on our social economic problems by bringing about economic evolution, rather than revolution. It is necessary for us to evolve in order to bring economic relief and stability to our national, and international, economies. Through economic evolution we can bring about an end to our desperate and debilitating need for taxes. While taxation has long been our sole social economic resource, it is now not only grossly inadequate but a social burden as well. Tax collections do not keep pace with our tax liability so our national and international debt is steadily growing. Our national debt is proof of our taxations systems inadequacy.

Since everyone agrees that their tax burden is unfair it's time for change. Taxes can be replaced by socially granted economic access to all social entities, including, the military, schools and hospitals, and state and local governments. Only granted access will be able to provide the social upkeep necessary to repair eighty thousand public schools across this nation, an estimated fifty billion dollar bill. Only granted access can repair the forty thousand bridges and half-million miles of highways across this nation, another seventy billion dollar bill. And only access can expand our infrastructure so that we don't live on top of each other. Only granted access can provide for our social upkeep and keep our wars from bankrupting our economy! Then government spending would be a boon to the economy instead of a burden.

The Congress of the United States of America must commit to ending economically motivated crime, the economic iniquities between the rich and poor, and all social problems that are part of the economic system we currently employ. They must strive to maintain the delicate balance which protects our value system, including the goal of reaching, and maintaining, an opulent life-style; while still allowing for the economic existence of less productive members of our society.

A strong society cannot afford the luxury of allowing charities and social programs to provide for its' members economic existence. We can no longer afford to allow the necessity of extracting from each other an economic existence. We must all have basic economic access in order to survive. It is evident that we cannot focus enough physical currency on any problem to alleviate the problem. Nor can we ensure an economic existence for every American from passing it around. As society becomes more complex we must make changes, not manipulations, in order to maintain a social order. The Congress of the United States of America will insure that our economic needs are met; through the use of our accounting technology. They will guide us as we make the transition from our cash based economic system, to a cashless economic system, and in the process, establish inalienable economic rights for the people of America.

Section II

We, the people of the Unites States of America, submit this amendment for change. It is our goal to accomplish, through this legislation, what hundreds of years of economic mismanagement, manipulation, and ambiguous economic strategy have not yet accomplished. That accomplishment will be the establishment of a self sustaining, people motivated and perpetual system of economics.

By establishing basic economic rights we will make economically motivated crime a bitter remembrance. If we build a hundred prison beds a day it will not solve the underlying economic problems causing the need for them.

We cannot continue to let our economic instability deny the very necessary elements of human economic existence to the millions who need it. We should no longer wait until an individual has reached rock bottom before trying to help them. It is economic desperation filling our prisons. It is hunger, and wanting for a better way of life, a better quality of life, that pushes would be children of God into economic situations, which wreak havoc with their lives.

We can no longer continue to amass astronomical personal fortunes while children go hungry and sleep in the street. To be a strong nation we must make it possible for every American to, not just believe in the American Dream, but to enjoy living it as well. Since we do not have the intestinal fortitude to place a ceiling on personal incomes there is only one way we can lessen the economic iniquity created by our dedication to capitalism. If income from a business can earn the owners, and key personal, millions of dollars a year in salary, then it should be illegal for their employees to require public assistance in order to remain economically viable. Once every voiceless American employee has been given enough economic access to establish and maintain life, then the wealthy can let their personal fortune grow. Let their personal access accumulate and multiply into billions for in the end they are just producers and users of what is produced. In ten lifetimes they will never spend their earnings. Income is just a measurement of our personal drive and ambition! Let them live, be merry, and pass their fortunes to their families when they die. But let not their fortunes cause a child to starve or go homeless.

Section III

The Congress of the United States of America is hereby charged, and empowered, to preserve the economic stability of our society and all that we believe in. We, the People of the United States of America, through this action, demand a stable, more equitable, and enriching economic existence for all Americans. An economic system without taxation, that furnishes the necessities of economic survival through established, earned or granted, economic access. We demand a system that is free of the economic stresses that are killing us or ruining our quality of life. We need to meet the goals, put forth by this amendment, which will enable us to deal with all the social-economic problems we face. We need a government committed to engineering the legislation to rid us of the currency based system we use, and all its' shortcomings. Being citizens of this country, we demand change.

With a vision, faith, and new economic theorem, it is our hope to heal the wounds, and stop the suffering inflicted on the people of America, solely because of the economy. We must stabilize and shore- up our economic foundation; bringing an end to the economic mayhem taking place in the world today. Then we can lead the way to easing the economic struggles, around the world; which trillions in tax and charitable dollars have not been able to lessen. The new economic direction proposed herein can address economic issues on an international scale and the blueprint, for the implementation of the changes proposed, can be easily understood.

Section IV

The Congress of the United States, in conjunction with business and financial institutions, will establish criteria for evaluating both commercial and individual levels of productivity. To oversee the authorization of accumulated productivity to access a National Economic Productivity and Access Bureau should be established, currently the IRS. The bureau should have federal and state government representatives along with business and civilian representatives; who will be responsible for outlining both business and individual levels of economic access; based upon:

A. The levels of productivity of both individuals and businesses

In everything we do there is a way of measuring the productivity that is necessary to accomplish a given task. As workers we can see how our level of productivity fits into the overall productivity of any business we are involved in. To establish our level of productivity we need to use three basic criteria:

a. Our level of responsibility in the company
b. Our salary or rate of pay
c. And the market performance of the business

B. The value of both individual and industrial productivity levels

The value of our productivity is something that is usually established by someone else. Many factors go into deciding how much of an economic reward is warranted for our labor. The decision is rarely made without bias. In essence we place some value on an individual's productive contribution to the process doing business. Showing how much economic access is earned, by an individual's productivity, can be achieved by looking, first, at the company's contribution to the Gross National Product in terms of billings. Then we can break it down to the individuals' contribution to that companies GDP. Since we can tell exactly how much any business in America makes, it is possible to pinpoint an individuals' access based upon the individuals' productive contribution to the business.

C. The longevity of an individuals' productivity

Presently, longevity accounts for very little unless it is amassed during service in one company. If an individual works long enough at one company he or she can realize the benefits of their longevity upon retirement. If an individual has many job changes, during the course of their work history, their benefits upon retirement will not compare with those of a person employed many years with one company. Continuing, legitimate productivity, no matter how it is distributed, should lead to economic advantages for the individual making the contributions. If a person contributes at the lowest level of productivity, throughout their work history, then their longevity should earn for them some of the benefits that their level of productivity didn't.

D. The legitimacy of the company and individual assets.

Since assets will determine both individual and company access it is important to scrutinize all company and individual holdings, particularly large amounts of undeclared physical currency. This will be done in order to deny high levels of economic access to individual~, or groups of individuals, that have amassed illegal fortunes. This day of reckoning will ensure that the economic access, to be granted to each person or group; has been earned by socially acceptable forms of productivity. Those who have obtained fortunes, through illegal means, will not be allowed to reap the benefits of an opulent life-style. We must not allow criminals to prosper from the pain and suffering their illegal activities wrought upon our society.

Congress, business, and financial leaders, through development of a National Economic Productivity and Access Bureau, will oversee the financial evaluations of both individuals and businesses. They will establish what the legitimate holdings of both individuals and businesses are, and establish economic access for both based upon those holdings. Congress and the National Economic Productivity and Access Bureau will investigate and hold hearings on the complaints of those being evaluated and granted access.

Section V

The Congress of the United States of America will delegate to existing financial institutions the responsibility of overseeing the transition from our current economic system, to that which operates with cashless access. The current tax offices will be responsible for issuing access cards to both individuals and businesses. Financial institutions will be responsible for tracking individual and business usage. They will track usage to prevent access abuses; and insure that appropriate access is being granted. The tax offices will raise or lower access based upon the evaluated productivity and usage of the individual, or business, being reported.

By using our technology we can ensure the financial recovery of our great nation, preserve our differences in life-styles, and establish economic rights for our people. By removing physical currency or system will operate not all that different from what transpires today. When going to buy a car most of us must get a loan. After a financial institutions' assessment of our income, and spending habits, the bank then decides how much of our productivity we have to spend on a car. Our ultimate purchase will be within the price range the bank sets for us.

The tax office will also be responsible for overseeing the eradication of all personal and public debts. Accounts receivables will be transferred into the access accounts of the receiving individuals and businesses due to receive them. That will wipe out the trillions of dollars of credit and debt that is owed by all individuals and businesses around the country. This is the only way to wipe the slate clean without seriously disrupting our lives. Everyone will be able to realize immediate benefits from access payments while no one will have to actually pay out anything. By having "the last pay day" we will be able to start over and never have to worry about debt and credit again.

Much of the technology needed to reform our economy is already in place. We can already make financial transactions without the use of physical currency. We can travel, build buildings, perform surgery, and provide every legitimate service imaginable without the use of physical currency. We must take our technology a step further and eliminate the need for physical currency in our everyday lives. We must now eliminate the need for physical currency when tipping, give gifts, or fulfilling any role as a medium for exchange.

The many positives benefits that will come from eliminating physical currency are easy to visualize. With no physical currency we will eliminate 98% of the crime and violence in our society. Crime and violence created by the need for, and struggle to obtain, the currency, that is now, essential to our survival. What we must do to stop a drug deal, stop prostitution, or stop any illegal activity is to eradicate the single tool used to sustain those practices and meet those demands; and that tool is physical currency.

We can, by making technological economic access our tool, ease the struggle for existence that has disrupted our social existence. Our overburdened legal system, bulging prisons, bulging social welfare programs, and bloated charities cry out for relief from the burdens of our inadequate economy. To stop the waste of human life it is necessary to bring quality and value to everyone's existence; allowing only personal drive and ambition, to make a difference in the lifestyles we are able to achieve and maintain. In keeping with our capitalist tradition a life-style of opulence will still be obtainable; and the unlimited personal access that some of us will reach, won't adversely affect the lives of the masses.

Section VI

The Congress of the United States of America will enact laws to change our system from wholesale and retail to one of distribution and usage; based on productivity and access. To purchase a house a real estate agent or brokerage will still be used. The buyer will go through an evaluation with the agent first, then a bank, to be qualified as to the value of the home they are able to have access to. Distribution of homes and apartments will make the housing industry more successful than it is now. Housing demands will go up as we all become home buyers or apartment dwellers, and the homeless situation will finally be laid to rest as we reach the goal of providing shelter for every member of our society. Grocery chains will become food distributors; then the plentiful resources of this earth won't rot on shelves instead of filling empty stomachs. Automobile dealerships will become distributorships, as cars are made available based upon the individuals reported level of productivity, employment longevity, and personal accessing power.

If there were not such a great economic disparity between the employer and employee fundamental changes in our economic structure would probably not be necessary. We have, however, reached a point where changes are not only necessary but also critically needed. An honest day's work should sustain the individual doing the work and take care of their basic economic needs. The fact that we have more working welfare recipients in this country is indicative of our failure to reach the goal of "an honest day's pay for an honest day's work."

Section VII

The Congress of the United States of America will turn America's vast army of tax collectors into a bureau with the responsibility of performing checks and balances for the businesses and individuals in our society. This is necessary to insure that business and individual productivity is properly recorded and our earned access is duly granted. Those who now keep track of our taxes will keep track of our individual productivity and usage, which is necessary to keep our level of economic access current. With the help of our existing financial institutions Congress will insure that economic access is granted to every citizen of the United States of America.

Our vast banking system is the other key to making this proposed financial system successful. In its' vast network, of computers and machines, lies all the answers we need to revitalize our financial existence; end welfare, and make positive changes. After installing their machines it will be the banks responsibility to ultimately eliminate any use of, or need for, physical currency. Our banking system can make all these things possible. Both our usage accountability, and our access balance, will be the responsibility of the same banks and financial institutions that we now entrust with similar responsibilities.

With these changes we can end world hunger. With these changes we can end the homeless situation facing millions. With these changes we can end debt (both social and private). The answer to our need for hundreds of trillions of tax dollars for our perpetual social upkeep does not lie in increased taxes. Economic access will make it possible to do many things that now have a prohibitive cost factor. With access we can run our government; both civilian and military, ease international suffering, and respond to natural disasters with positive action; both here and abroad. With access we can provide free education for everyone who wants it. With access we can easily pump water to the desert or make use of alternative energy. With access we can do everything that cost factors have kept us from doing. We have the technology; we have the minds, to make these changes work. Only God could make a perfect plan; but as His children we should be able to come close to His perfection. Without change we have little chance to prevail against the demands placed on our limited financial resources. Our economy is an overwhelming force upon our physical existence and when it fails to whom shall we turn? With the rest of the world already going door-to-door, with their hands out, it is not hard to see that this could be the beginning of our economic end; if not the end of life, as we know it. Take a lesson from history. People are not going to starve without putting up a fight. It is time for change. The great French revolution proved that as the voices of the poor cry out neither wealth, nor armies, will keep the repressed from rising up.

Any government that fails to address the concerns of its' citizenry may be rendered extinct. If we entrench ourselves in a failing ecosystem the human race is in for very hard times. If we are smart enough to adapt and/or evolve, we can survive. None of us should have to guess when or where our next meal is coming from. None of us should have to wonder the streets at night or waste away in overcrowded prisons. Only economic rights can change the course of America.

Section VIII

We the People of the United States of America do hereby charge the Congress of the United States of America to fulfill the duty they have been elected to perform and secure the freedoms we elected them to preserve. We demand:

a. A society free of debt

b. A society free of homeless

c. A society free of hunger

d. A society free of crime and drugs

e. A healthy society

f. A poverty free society

g. An educated society

Or we want them to resign and step aside for those of us who can solve the economic problems of the world. America is in need of vision! If our leaders do not have enough vision to see that further manipulations of our failed acquisition based economic system cannot resuscitate it; then I ask them to please step aside before more prisons are needed, blood is shed, or lives are destroyed and lost.

ABOUT THE AUTHOR

My name is Lenard Latimer, Jr. I am a husband, father, grandfather, brother, citizen of the world, and the founder and chairman of the P.O.W.E.R.S. organization.

The quest that I am on started in 1975 when money first became a problem for me. Being broke is a common problem, but the affects it has on fragile human lives can be traumatic. Money problems are bad for the rich and the poor. As a young military brat, and Airman, I traveled the world and learned what poverty and suffering were up close and personal. From the rice paddies of Japan to the barrios of the Philippines and to countless cities across America, I grew up looking poverty square in the face. Then it hit home! I'm not going to go into detail but suffice it to say that a temporary brush with poverty changed my life forever.

I also saw what money is doing to us. It is a powerful force, and even powerful foe, able to turn a mothers against their children, brothers against brothers, husbands against wives, and countries against countries! Money does not buy the important things in life. Happiness, security, or love. But it does rule our world! I saw people worship money more than the people around them. Not just for the sake of personal security, but because they have adopted a position that everyone should stand on their own.

I once heard a prosecutor say, when he found himself in prison for breaking a law, that if he knew what prison was like he would never have sentenced anyone to the draconian sentences he had asked the court to impose on people. Wealthy people fear being poor. Those who live to experience poverty, are more likely to take their life rather than live below the standard to which they have imposed upon others by paying wages so low that they deny all their employees anything but a life of struggle without hope.

My mother and father taught me differently! They created sort of a paradox in my life. My father taught me to be strong, independent, and to be weary and suspicious of the people in the world. He was disappointed that I became a bleeding heart liberal, caring too much about my fellow man. He hated that I sometimes helped others to the point where I sometimes needed help myself. He knew I could do much better if I cared less about other people. He was a retired military Baptist minister who was intolerant of people of other religions.

My mother, on the other hand, taught me how to disarm people with politeness and a smile when I walked into a room. Because I was six foot one inch tall in the ninth grade and weighed 190 pounds she wanted to make sure that people did not perceive me as a threat because of my size. She taught me to defend the weak, that my size and might did not make me right, and to help others and give to the poor! My mother won out! When I realized that I could not help the world out of my own pocket, God, my Father, gave me the answers I sought to help mankind move beyond poverty, hunger, and all the problems caused by our failed acquisition based system of economics; and I am giving them to you. As it says in Re:1:11: Saying, I am Alpha and Omega, the first and the last: and, What thou sees, write in a book, and send it unto the seven churches which are in Asia; unto Ephesus, and unto Smyrna, and unto Pergamos, and unto Thyatira, and unto Sardis, and unto Philadelphia, and unto Laodicea. I have done as I was asked!

www.ingramcontent.com/pod-product-compliance
Lightning Source LLC
Chambersburg PA
CBHW051329170526
45166CB00002B/738